Pot Pies

Hobby Farm Home® Presents
Volume 10K · 2013

Senior Associate Editor
Annika Small

Editor in Chief
Amy K. Hooper

Associate Art Director
Kari Keegan

Multimedia Production Coordinator
Leah Rosalez

Multimedia Production Manager
Jessica Jaensch

Contributing Photographers
Wendy Bedwell-Wilson, Ashley English, Kevin Fogle,
Fiona Green, Daniel Johnson, Kyra Kirkwood,
Patricia Lehnhardt, Rhoda Peacher, Alexander Small

Editorial, Production and Sales Office
3 Burroughs
Irvine CA 92618-2804
949-855-8822;
fax: 949-855-3045

Sales Offices
500 N. Brand Blvd., Suite 600
Glendale CA 91203
213-385-2222;
fax: 213-385-0335

477 Butterfield, Suite 200
Lombard IL 60148
630-515-9493;
fax: 630-515-9784

POT PIES has been published by I-5 Publishing, 3 Burroughs,
Irvine, CA 92618-2804. Corporate headquarters is located at
3 Burroughs, Irvine, CA 92618-2804.

i-5 publishing
Imagination • Innovation
Insight • Inspiration • Integrity

MARK HARRIS, Chief Executive Officer; NICOLE FABIAN, Chief
Financial Officer; JEFF SCHARF, Chief Sales Officer; JUNE
KIKUCHI, Chief Content Officer; BETH FREEMAN REYNOLDS, Vice
President, Consumer Marketing; MELISSA KAUFFMAN, Digital
General Manager; LISA MACDONALD, Marketing Director; LAURIE
PANAGGIO, Multimedia Production Director; CHRISTOPHER REG-
GIO, Book Division General Manager; CRAIG WISDA, Controller;
CHARLES LEE, IT Director; CHERRI BUCHANAN, Human Resources
Director; PAM THOMAS, Administration and Facility Director

Registration Number: R126851765
Part of the Hobby Farm Home® Presents Series
Printed in the USA

Life of Pie

BY ANNIKA SMALL

When we began planning which recipes to share with you, I found several definitions for the term "pot pie." According to Merriam-Webster's online dictionary, a pot pie is "a meat and veg-etables that is co... ... ...ooked in a deep dish." Elino... ... ...umminess in a Dish" (Chroni... ... ...at pot pies' "common thread is that they ... ...ooking methods." One of our frequent contributors, Cheryl Morrison, writes in her article on page 4 that most "pot pies have crusts that encase — or at least cover — stewlike fillings."

Faced with these varied opinions, I wasn't sure which rec-ipes to include. Should they all include meat and vegetables? What about crust? Are pot pies main courses to be served only at lunch or dinner, or do people eat them at other times of the day? Can pot pies taste sweet — or just savory?

Ultimately, we decided to embrace nontraditional versions. We've included recipes for chicken (pages 23 and 26), turkey (pages 20 and 22), beef (page 30) and vegetable (page 41) pot pies — all of your favorite comfort-food classics. You'll also find recipes for unusual pies, such as shepherd's pie (page 28), five-cheese pizza pot pie (page 44), lobster pot pie (page 47), savory vegan pot pie with tofu and potatoes (page 56), breakfast-sausage-hash pot pie (page 63), apricot and almond baklava (page 78), and many more. Plus, we've got tips about pairing these dishes with beer (page 90).

One thing these recipes have in com-mon besides their de-liciousness: They all feature some sort of crust. (You'll find rec-ipes for *that* on page 14.) We'll leave it to you to flip through the following pages and decide whether, in your opinion, that of-ficially qualifies them as pot pies or not. En-joy your "research"!

ALEXANDER SMALL

Pot Pies

28

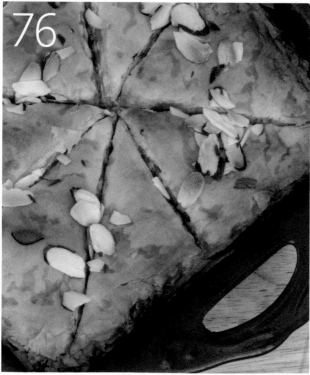

76

38

COVER IMAGE BY bonchan/ Shutterstock

Difficult to Define, Easy to Make

The humble pot pie comes filled with a fascinating history.

BY CHERYL MORRISON

Pot-pie toppings aren't limited to pie crust.
Shepherd's pie comes covered with mashed potatoes.

when
you hear the term "pot pie," you might have a specific dish in mind. For me, it's the Pennsylvania-Dutch style of chicken pot pie that I grew up eating — tender chunks of chicken, potatoes, carrots and onion plus thick, chewy egg noodles in a silken broth seasoned with nothing more than salt and pepper.

My family's chicken pot pie is cooked in a pot, and it does involve dough (for the noodles), but it is actually a stew rather than a pie. Other types of pot pies are not cooked in pots; instead, they are baked in pie pans, Dutch ovens or casserole dishes. If your definition of "pot pie" includes Mexican empanadas, Cornish pasties and other regional foods wrapped in or covered with pastry, then pot pies also can be baked on cookie sheets.

Except for the Pennsylvania-Dutch version, pot pies have crusts that encase — or at least cover — stewlike fillings. The fillings usually combine vegetables — often root vegetables, such as onions, potatoes and carrots — with meat or fish. Some omit the vegetables, though, and some use only meat.

Pot-pie crust is usually made with flour, but the cooking website Epicurious.com features a recipe for halibut pot pie with a covering of mashed potatoes. If that dish qualifies as a pot pie, so does shepherd's pie, which generally has a mashed-potato crust.

Frequent Fillings

Meat can include poultry, beef, lamb, pork and fish. The meat might be cooked before it goes into the pie — or it might not.

Pot pies generally are simple, although few are as simple as a recipe in my 60-year-old copy of "The Joy of Cooking" (Scribner) for "Canned Stew Pot Pie." It calls for dumping a 20-ounce can of "stew: beef, lamb, etc." into an ovenproof pot; covering it with pie dough, biscuit dough or slices of bread buttered on both sides; and baking it at 400 degrees Fahrenheit until the covering appears light brown. (Mercifully, the authors — Irma S. Rombauer and Marion Rombauer Becker — omitted this recipe from subsequent editions.)

A later edition of the same classic cookbook contains a chicken pot-pie recipe that starts with stewing a whole chicken and making 3 cups of gravy. The meat and gravy go into a baking dish. You then make a batter of flour, eggs, milk, salt, baking powder and butter; pour the batter over the meat and gravy; and bake it at 375 degrees F until light brown. The recipe notes that the crust

Root vegetables — including onions, potatoes and carrots — often play a starring role in vegetarian pot pies.

KAI KEISUKE/SHUTTERSTOCK

The term "pot pie" **originated in England,** where cooks baked meats in "coffins" that they formed by molding pastry to fit inside a pot or pie pan.

Cut filling ingredients into bite-sized pieces before adding to a pot pie.

will "soak up quite a bit" of the gravy. "Some cooks," it says, "prefer a biscuit pie crust top that is cut to fit the casserole, baked separately and adjusted while hot over the cooked chicken."

Rombauer and Becker also note that meat pies can be "an agreeable disposition of refrigerator accumulations." Indeed, nearly any combination of vegetables — with or without leftover meat or fish — can be stirred with a little gravy or simple sauce, covered with pie dough, and baked into a tasty, nutritious dinner without much fuss.

American and English pot-pie recipes typically call for fillings seasoned with nothing stronger than mild herbs so the flavor comes mainly from the meat and vegetables themselves. Recipes from other locales are more apt to use spices and other ingredients with stronger flavors. The sfeeha (Arabic meat pastry), for example, uses cinnamon and cardamom to season the lamb and tomato filling, which is baked in an open pastry. The seasonings in bstilla, a Moroccan pigeon pie, include saffron, ginger and allspice. Empanadas often contain chorizo, a sausage (usually pork) made with chili peppers that can be *muy picante* (very spicy!).

Varied as they are, pot pies do have at least two traits in common:

• Pot pies are savory, which distinguishes them from fruit pies, cream pies, turnovers and other sweet pastries.
• Their fillings consist of bite-sized pieces of meat, fish or vegetables — or vegetables combined with meat or fish — bathed in broth or gravy.

Cheryl Morrison splits her time between New York City and southern Vermont.

A miniature pot pie makes a delicious one-person meal.

From Rome to Mexico, via England

Pot pies of one kind or another have appeared on menus around the world for at least 2,000 years, taking on many shapes and flavors. Their popularity throughout America owes much to the British.

Banquet tables in the Roman Empire often featured pot pies. "Apicius: Cookery and Dining in Imperial Rome" (Dover Publications) contains a recipe for ham cooked with laurel leaves and figs and covered with a crust before baking. As the Romans expanded their empire to the north and east, they exported their taste for meat pies.

The rascally Romans sometimes baked pies containing live birds, which would fly out to startle dinner guests when the pies were cut. The Italians and British carried on with the joke. Iona and Peter Opie's "The Oxford Dictionary of Nursery Rhymes" (Oxford University Press) cites a 16th century Italian cookbook that included instructions for making pies "so that birds may be alive in them and file out when it is cut up." That cookbook was soon translated into English. Its presence in English kitchens suggests that "Sing a Song of Sixpence" — the nursery rhyme about "four and twenty blackbirds baked in a pie" so that "when the pie was opened the birds began to sing" — was no mere nonsense verse.

Meat pies became something of a fad among English gentry during the 16th century. One British food writer of that time remarked on the English

preference for making them from venison. In her book "Pies: Recipes, History, Snippets" (Ebury Press), Joan Struthers says the term "humble pie" derives from a once-popular English dish made of umbles, a term for the innards of deer. The gentry feasted on pies made with the choicest deer flesh, and their servants tucked into pies made of umbles. Another popular British savory from bygone days was the eel pie.

The term "pot pie" originated in England, where cooks baked meats in "coffins" that they formed by molding pastry to fit inside a pot or pie pan.

At a tin mine in Cornwall, England, that I once visited, the tour guide talked about the Cornish pasty (pronounced *pahs-tee*) as a hand-held convenience food for miners in days past. Wives would bake the semicircular meat pies daily and lower them into the mineshafts at mealtime. The dough for pasty crust is folded over the filling to form a semicircle, with its edges pinched together to seal in the contents and create a thick, tough seam. Miners ate the pasties with their grimy hands, holding them by the seams to avoid soiling the tender part of the crust, and discarding the seams when they finished eating.

According to the tour guide, Mexicans began to make empanadas, which outwardly are nearly identical to pasties, after Cornishmen sailed to Mexico during the early 1800s to work in the mines. — *C.M.*

Cornish pasties look similar to empanadas and are filled with meat and vegetables.

BRATWUSTLE/SHUTTERSTOCK

Investing in Stocks

BY CHERYL MORRISON

Prepare today for your pot-pie-making future with simple recipes for chicken, beef and vegetable stocks.

vegetable, chicken and beef stocks serve as the bases for innumerable soups, stews and sauces. You can make stocks at home that are tastier, more healthful and less expensive than most commercial brands. Some stocks must simmer for hours, but the active preparation time from start to stovetop takes only a few minutes.

Vegetable Stock

Vegetable stocks require less simmering time than those that include meat. You can make a flavorful stock using only vegetables, garlic and a sachet of common herbs and spices. Vegetable stock can replace chicken stock to produce delicious pot pies. As with all stocks, you can add or subtract ingredients and adjust their quantities to suit your taste buds. A meatless stock such as this one can provide the basis for countless vegetarian and vegan dishes.

1 bay leaf
1½ tsp. fresh thyme leaves or ½ tsp. dried thyme
3 or 4 parsley sprigs
3 or 4 whole black peppercorns
1 whole clove
1 medium red or yellow onion, peeled
1 medium leek (including the white bulb and the green stem), rinsed thoroughly
1 celery rib, leaves included
1 carrot, peeled
half a tomato
2 Tbsp. vegetable oil

3 garlic cloves, peeled and crushed
1 gallon cold water

1 Tie the bay leaf, thyme, parsley, peppercorns and clove into a double layer of cheesecloth to make a sachet. Chop the onion, leek, celery, carrot and tomato.

2 In a heavy-bottomed stockpot over medium heat, cook the oil. Lower the heat, add all of the vegetables and the garlic, cover, and cook for about 5 minutes or until the onions become translucent and a little soft but not browned.

3 Pour the cold water over the vegetables, drop the sachet of herbs into the pot, and turn up the heat to high. When the vegetable stock reaches a boil, lower the heat, and simmer for 45 minutes.

4 Remove the stock from the heat, strain it, and discard the solid ingredients.

Chicken Stock

There are as many variations on chicken stock as there are cooks who make it. Some stock recipes use only chicken, vegetables and a few herbs, simmered slowly in water with a little salt and pepper. Others call for ginger, cloves or other flavorings.

Bones create the difference between a rich stock and a delicate broth — one that's made without bones — and the meat and bones can be cooked or fresh. Some cooks choose to use the leftover carcasses of roasted chickens, with meat scraps still clinging to the bones, which can keep in the freezer until ready to make stock. Others use fresh chicken, which needn't be young or tender, because the meat gets discarded. All that matters is flavor. You can experiment with variations on this basic recipe to develop a version that's all your own.

TRAVELLIGHT/SHUTTERSTOCK

1 large carrot or 2 small ones
1 large onion with peel
1 Tbsp. vegetable oil
3 celery stalks
1 bay leaf
10 whole peppercorns
1 gallon cold water
salt to taste (optional)

1. Cut the chicken into pieces; reserve the bones. Note that the chicken heart and gizzard are excellent for use in stocks. Set aside the liver for another purpose, though; stock made with liver can become murky and unappetizing.

2. Wash but do not peel the carrot, and cut it into chunks. Quarter the unpeeled onion.

3. In a large stockpot, heat the oil, add the chicken parts, and cook them for a few minutes to brown the skin. Add the remaining ingredients to the pot, and slowly bring the liquid to a boil.

4. Turn the heat to low, and simmer the stock, skimming the foam from the surface every half-hour. Keep the stock simmering, uncovered, for at least 2½ hours — until the chicken is so thoroughly cooked that it falls from the bones and easily can be pulled apart with a fork.

5. Strain the liquid, and discard the solid ingredients. Add salt to taste.

Preserving Stock: Shelf Versus Freezer

Chicken, beef and vegetable stock will keep for many months when canned or frozen. Both preservation methods produce excellent results, and you will have homemade stock at the ready for weeks or months to come.

For both methods, start by refrigerating the stock until the fat rises and congeals; then skim the fat from the surface. If you choose to can the stock, reheat it while you sterilize the jars.

For canned stock, you must use a pressure canner. Follow the instructions for your particular canner and altitude. Unlike pickles, chutneys and acidic fruits and vegetables, stocks cannot be safely preserved with a boiling-water bath — the most common canning method.

Pressure canning your stock requires some time and trouble, but it offers these advantages over freezing:

- When you're ready to use the stock, you need only open a jar. Thawing time isn't necessary.
- Canned stock requires no freezer space, and there's no danger of spoilage if the power goes out in your home.

Freezing stock requires only these simple steps once the fat is removed:

- Pour the stock into clean plastic containers, leaving 1 inch of headroom, because the stock will expand as it freezes.
- Fasten the lids tightly to the containers, and stack the containers in the freezer.

Freezing stocks and other liquids in glass jars is not recommended, because jars are highly prone to breakage as liquid expands into the narrow areas at the tops of the jars.

You can use pint- and quart-sized containers for any stock that you plan to use specifically in those quantities, but smaller containers often are handy if you require smaller amounts of stock for other purposes, such as making sauces or glazes. — C.M.

TIP

If you freeze some stock in ice-cube trays and then transfer the frozen stock cubes to a plastic bag, you can pull a cube from the bag when a recipe calls for just a tablespoon or two of stock.

MOVING MOMENT/SHUTTERSTOCK

Beef Stock

Roasting beef, bones and vegetables in the oven before combining them with liquid produces a rich stock with a deep brown color. The oven heat caramelizes the vegetables, adding flavor to the stock. You can use this stock as the basis for classic French onion soup as well as numerous dishes and sauces.

5 lb. meaty beef bones, preferably including some knuckle bones, with some marrow exposed
1 lb. chuck, flank or scraps
1 large onion, unpeeled
2 medium carrots
olive oil as needed
1 cup hot water
1 celery stalk
3 unpeeled garlic cloves, crushed
6 fresh parsley sprigs
2 bay leaves
10 peppercorns
3 quarts cold water

1 Preheat the oven to 400 degrees Fahrenheit. Cut the meat into 2-inch chunks. Quarter the unpeeled onion, wash but do not peel the carrots, and cut the carrots and celery into 1-inch pieces.

Rub the beef bones with olive oil — enough to coat the bones.

2 Using a large pan, roast the bones, meat, onion and carrots in the oven for about 45 minutes, turning from time to time until they are brown. Transfer to a large stockpot.

3 Heat the roasting pan on the stovetop over low heat, add hot water to the pan, and scrape it with a metal spatula to loosen browned meat that sticks to the bottom.

4 Pour the liquid from the roasting pan, along with any bits of meat, into the stockpot.

5 Add the celery, garlic, parsley, bay leaves and peppercorns to the stockpot with enough cold water just to cover the bones. Slowly bring the liquid to a boil; then simmer, uncovered, for about 5 hours.

6 Strain the liquid through a cheesecloth-lined sieve. Discard the solid ingredients, which will have imparted their flavor to the stock.

Crust Recipes

BY SHARON KEBSCHULL BARRETT

pot-pie crusts are generally interchangeable, so don't be afraid to work with whatever you have on hand. These easy recipes include individual baking guidelines — especially useful for cooks who improvise a filling by, say, folding leftover roasted vegetables into a simple sauce. You won't go wrong, however, with any pot-pie crust if you bake it at 400 to 425 degrees Fahrenheit for 30 to 45 minutes for a golden crust and bubbly filling. If the crust darkens too quickly, lay a piece of foil over the top, reduce the heat to 375 degrees F, and/or move the pie to the bottom shelf of the oven.

All crusts look more appetizing if glazed before baking; try topping a glazed crust with poppy or sesame seeds, grated Parmesan or large-grained salt if the filling isn't salty. Take heart! These forgiving crusts make pot pies possible even for last-minute suppers.

All-purpose Pot-pie Crust

Use very cold or even slightly frozen butter and cream cheese in this recipe. If you don't have cream cheese on hand, just use butter. To make this without a food processor, cut the butter and cream cheese into the flour with a pastry blender (aka pastry cutter) or, working quickly, with your fingertips; then gently stir in the liquid ingredients. Two tricks to making the dough into a circle: Roll the dough from the center to the edge; then give it a one-third turn — not a quarter turn, which leads you to a square. After the dough is rolled out, you can even the edge by running a knife around a large pizza pan or other plate laid on top. You don't need to chill the dough before rolling it out; chill it after rolling if possible.

Yields 1 9-inch double crust: enough for 12 6-inch circles to top individual pie pans or ramekins; to cover 2 oval casserole dishes; or to cover 2 9-inch square dishes

2¼ cups unbleached all-purpose flour
½ tsp. fine salt (preferably sea salt)

6 oz. very cold, unsalted butter (1½ sticks; use 1¾ sticks if not using cream cheese)
2 oz. very cold cream cheese, cut into about 8 pieces
1 Tbsp. white or cider vinegar
⅓ cup iced water or more as needed
Glaze: 2 Tbsp. half-and-half or cream or 1 beaten egg; poppy or sesame seeds; grated Parmesan cheese; or large-grained salt (optional)

1 In a food processor, mix the flour and salt. Halve the sticks of butter lengthwise, turn a quarter turn, and halve again; then make 8 cuts crosswise to cube. Add 1 stick of butter and the cream cheese to the food processor. Pulse just until the mixture resembles coarse meal.

2 Add the remaining butter, and pulse again 8 times — until the butter looks cut in but some pea-size chunks remain visible.

KEVIN FOGLE

3 Add the vinegar and 6 Tbsp. water, and pulse just until the dough starts to look crumbly — not until it forms a ball. Squeeze a bit of the dough between your fingertips; if it does not hold together, add 1 Tbsp. water, and pulse a few more times. Repeat if needed.

4 Turn out the dough onto a lightly floured rolling board, and gently press into 2 disks, and pat them smooth.

5 Use a lightly floured rolling pin to roll out one disk to ¼ inch thick and 1 inch bigger in diameter than your baking dish; trim the edges into a rough circle if they appear very uneven. If you have time, place the dough on a baking sheet and chill, covered in plastic, for at least 30 minutes and up to 2 days. This allows the gluten to relax and the butter to chill so the dough holds its shape during baking. Repeat with the remaining disk.

6 If you wish to make a pot pie with top and bottom crusts, fold one crust in half, and transfer it to a baking dish, unfolding and gently tucking it into the corners of the dish without stretching. Add the filling. Take the remaining dough, fold it in half, lay it on top of the filling, unfold, and tuck the edge under the bottom crust. Flute the edge or press in a pattern with the tines of a fork. If you prefer a top-crust-only pot pie, simply lay the dough atop the filling, tuck the edge under, and flute.)

7 Lightly brush the dough with half-and-half or cream or a beaten egg. Sprinkle with poppy or sesame seeds, grated Parmesan or large-grained salt if the filling isn't salty.

8 Bake according to the recipe directions.

Whole-wheat Pot-pie Crust

Making a flaky whole-wheat crust works best with a combination of all-purpose flour and white whole-wheat flour, now widely available in grocery stores and online. Make the crust the first time using the following proportions; as you get more comfortable with the recipe, try increasing the proportion of whole-wheat to all-purpose flour — up to about 1½ cups white whole-wheat.

Yields 1 9-inch double crust: enough for 12 6-inch circles to top individual pie pans or ramekins; to cover 2 oval casserole dishes; or to cover 2 9-inch square dishes

1 cup unbleached all-purpose flour
1 cup white whole-wheat flour
½ tsp. fine salt (preferably sea salt)
½ tsp. baking powder
6 oz. very cold, unsalted butter (1½ sticks)
2 Tbsp. fresh lemon juice
6 to 8 Tbsp. iced water or more as needed
Glaze: 2 Tbsp. half-and-half or cream or 1 beaten egg; poppy or sesame seeds, grated Parmesan cheese or large-grained salt (optional)

1 In a food processor, mix the flours, salt and baking powder. Halve the sticks of butter lengthwise, turn a quarter turn, and halve again; then make 8 cuts crosswise to cube.

2 Add about 1 stick of butter to the processor. Pulse just until the mixture resembles coarse meal. Add the remaining butter, and pulse 8 times — until cut in but with some pea-size chunks still visible.

3 Add the lemon juice and 6 Tbsp. water; pulse just until the dough starts to look crumbly — not until it forms a ball. Squeeze a bit of the dough between your fingertips; if it does not hold together, sprinkle in 1 Tbsp. water, and pulse a few more times. Repeat if needed.

4 Turn out the dough onto a lightly floured board, and gently press into 2 disks; pat them smooth.

5 Use a lightly floured rolling pin to roll out one disk to ¼ inch thick and about 1 inch bigger in diameter than your baking dish; trim the edges into a rough circle if they look uneven. If you have time, place the dough on a baking sheet and chill, covered in plastic, for at least 30 minutes and up to 2 days. Repeat with the remaining disk.

6 To make a pot pie with top and bottom crusts, fold one crust in half, transfer it to the baking dish of your choice, and unfold, gently tucking it into the corners without stretching. Add the filling. Take the remaining dough, fold it in half, lay it on top of the filling, unfold, and tuck the edge under the bottom crust. Flute the edge or press in a pattern with the tines of a fork. (For a top-crust pot pie, simply lay the dough atop the filling, tuck the edge under, and flute.)

7 Lightly brush the dough with half-and-half or cream or a beaten egg. Sprinkle with poppy or sesame seeds, grated Parmesan or large-grained salt if the filling is not salty. Bake according to the recipe directions.

STEPHANIE FREY/SHUTTERSTOCK

Cream Biscuit Pot-pie Crust ////////////////////////////////////

Easy and somewhat lower in fat than buttermilk biscuits, cream biscuits make an ideal pot-pie topping. Try adding grated cheese, fresh or dried herbs, seeds or ground nuts as appropriate for your filling. If you want flakier biscuits, cut 2 to 4 Tbsp. unsalted butter into the flour mixture. These work best if your filling is at least warm — if not hot. If you have extra biscuits, bake them on a greased or parchment-lined baking sheet at 425 degrees F for about 12 minutes or until golden.

Yields 15 2½-inch biscuits, 1 9-inch pot pie, 1 9-by-13-inch casserole dish, or enough dough to cover 12 ramekins

2 cups unbleached all-purpose flour
1 Tbsp. baking powder
½ tsp. fine salt, preferably sea salt, or ½ tsp. coarse (kosher) salt
1¼ cups heavy cream or more as needed for dough and glaze, if using
Optional add-ins: 2 tsp. minced fresh herb leaves; 1 tsp. dried herb leaves; 1½ Tbsp. poppy seeds or sesame seeds; ½ to 1 Tbsp. freshly ground pepper; ½ cup freshly grated Parmesan or other hard cheese; ¾ to 1 cup grated Cheddar or other semisoft cheese; and/or ⅓ cup ground, toasted nuts

1 In a medium bowl, thoroughly whisk the flour, baking powder and salt. If using any add-ins, whisk them in now.

2 Add the cream, and stir it in with a spatula; add more cream by tablespoons if necessary for the dough to hold together.

3 Turn out the dough onto a lightly floured board, and gently press together into a ball. Use a lightly floured rolling pin to press or roll out the dough into a ¾-inch-thick circle.

4 Cut into 2- or 3-inch rounds with a lightly floured biscuit cutter or drinking glass, pressing straight down and back up. Don't twist the cutter.

5 Place the biscuits atop your filling, spacing slightly apart. If you prefer, glaze them by brushing lightly with cream. Follow the recipe directions, or bake at 425 degrees F for 15 to 30 minutes until the filling is bubbly and the biscuits are golden.

Rough Puff Pastry

This super-fast puff pastry, sometimes called "blitz puff pastry," relies on sour cream for its flakiness and puffiness without the multiple folds of a traditional puff pastry. Some recipes give it an extra boost by adding up to ½ tsp. baking powder to the flour and salt. Note that the puff pastry needs at least 2 hours of chilling time; make sure to bake it long enough to become dark-golden and crisp.

Yields 1 generous pound — enough to roll into a 12-by-24-inch rectangle

1 ½ cups all-purpose flour
½ tsp. fine salt (preferably sea salt)
8 oz. very cold, unsalted butter (2 sticks), each stick cut into 16 pieces
½ cup sour cream
Glaze: 1 beaten egg

1. In a food processor, mix the flour and salt. Add the butter, and pulse just enough to cut in the butter until the mixture resembles coarse crumbs. (To do this by hand, whisk the flour and salt in a large bowl; then cut in the butter with a pastry blender or two knives.)

2. Transfer the dough to a medium bowl, and stir in the sour cream with a spatula; the mixture will seem dry. Press and knead the dough very lightly until it just holds together. Gather into a disk, and wrap tightly with plastic wrap. Refrigerate for at least 2 hours or up to 3 days.

3. On a lightly floured surface, roll out half or all of the dough to the desired size. The dough will be very stiff. If you have time, you can give it one or two folds: Fold the dough in thirds like a letter, give it a quarter turn, and roll it out again, letting the dough rest briefly in the refrigerator if it resists rolling out. (Give it one more fold if you like; this increases the flakiness).

4. Fold the dough in half, lay it over the filling, unfold, and tuck any edges into the side of the pan.

5. Brush gently with the egg, preventing the egg from dripping down the sides, and bake according to the filling directions (or at 425 degrees F) until the pastry looks deeply golden and crisp and the filling is bubbly — at least 25 minutes.

Poultry Pies

RECIPES AND PHOTOS BY PATRICIA LEHNHARDT

whether you use chicken, turkey or duck, poultry pot pies make delicious comfort food.

Turkey Mole Pie

The rich, spicy chocolate flavor of mole is always a hit. While the ingredient list is long, the complexity of texture and taste proves worth the effort. This recipe makes a perfect use for leftover turkey after a holiday feast when everyone craves a change.

Serves 6

1 Tbsp. olive oil
1 medium onion, diced (1 cup)
1 small red bell pepper, diced (1 cup)
¼ cup tomato paste
2 garlic cloves, minced

1 Tbsp. ancho chili powder
½ tsp. chipotle chili powder
½ tsp. anise seed
½ tsp. ground cinnamon
½ tsp. dried marjoram
1 Tbsp. sesame seeds
2 Tbsp. cocoa powder
3 Tbsp. dried cranberries
3 cups turkey stock
2½ cups cubed, cooked turkey
1 cup corn kernels
1 cup cooked black beans
2 Tbsp. masa flour
cornbread biscuits (recipe to the left)
3 Tbsp. pumpkin seeds

1 Preheat the oven to 400 degrees Fahrenheit. In a large sauté pan, heat the oil. Add the onion and bell pepper, and sauté until softened.

2 Add the tomato paste, garlic, spices and cocoa. Cook for 1 minute, stirring constantly to brown the spices and tomato paste. Stir in the cranberries and stock. Simmer for at least 20 to 30 minutes.

3 Stir in the turkey, corn and black beans. Bring the mixture to a boil. Add the masa, and mix. Cook for 1 or 2 minutes until the sauce thickens. Pour everything into a 1½-quart casserole dish. Top with dollops of cornmeal biscuits, sprinkle with pumpkin seeds, and bake for 20 minutes until the biscuits appear golden and the filling bubbles. Serve immediately.

Cornbread Drop Biscuits

1 cup cornmeal
¼ cup all-purpose flour
1 tsp. baking powder
½ tsp. baking soda
¼ tsp. salt
1 egg
½ cup buttermilk
2 Tbsp. melted butter

In a medium bowl, combine the cornmeal, flour, baking powder, baking soda and salt. In another bowl, whisk the egg, buttermilk and melted butter together. Stir the wet ingredients into the dry ingredients, just until blended.

TIP Reheat at 350 degrees F, uncovered, for 25 minutes.

Thanksgiving Turkey Pot Pie //

The perfect vehicle for leftovers, this pie will satisfy when you need a taste of Thanksgiving. You can even substitute roast chicken — but don't tell anyone.

Serves 6 to 8

2½ cups shredded, roasted turkey

Dressing
1 Tbsp. butter
¼ cup onion, diced
¼ cup celery, diced
2 slices whole-wheat toast, cut into ½-inch cubes
½ tsp. poultry seasoning
¼ cup turkey stock

Green beans
½ cup diced cremini mushrooms
2 cups thin green beans, cut into 1-inch pieces
½ cup turkey stock

Onions
½ medium onion, thinly sliced
2 Tbsp. all-purpose flour
½ cup peanut oil

Sauce
2½ cups turkey stock
¼ cup cream
½ tsp. poultry seasoning
salt and pepper to taste
3 Tbsp. cornstarch mixed with 3 Tbsp. water

Assembly
double-crust pastry (see page 14)
egg wash: 1 egg whisked with 1 Tbsp. water

1 Melt the butter in a small skillet, and sauté the onion and celery until soft. Transfer to a small bowl, and stir in the toast, poultry seasoning and stock. Mix well to moisten the toast.

2 In a small pot, combine the mushrooms, green beans and stock. Bring to a boil, lower the heat, cover, and simmer for 3 to 4 minutes until the beans are just tender. Drain.

3 Toss the onion slices with the flour to coat. Heat the oil in a small pot until it shimmers (350 degrees F). Add the onions in 3 batches. Stir until golden-brown and crisp — 3 to 4 minutes. Remove with tongs, and drain on paper towels.

4 In a medium pot, bring the stock and cream to a boil. Add the poultry seasoning, salt and pepper. Whisk in the cornstarch mixture, and cook 1 to 2 minutes, whisking constantly until thickened.

5 Preheat the oven to 375 degrees F. Roll out the bottom crust, and fit it into a 10-inch deep-dish pie plate. Trim to the edge of the dish. Layer the turkey, dressing, beans and fried onions. Pour the sauce evenly over the top.

6 Roll out the second half of the pastry, and lay on top of the filling. Trim to ½ inch beyond the edge, tuck the top pastry under the bottom, and crimp the edges to seal the two together.

7 Cut vents with a sharp paring knife, and brush with half of the egg wash. Decorate with pastry scraps cut into shapes, if desired, and brush again with egg wash. Bake for 1 hour or until the crust looks golden and the filling bubbles out of the vents.

Chicken Pot Pie

Traditional chicken pie fancied up a bit with wine and bacon, this family favorite is perfect to warm up a chilly evening.

Serves 6 to 8

2 slices thick-cut bacon
1 lb. boneless, skinless chicken thighs or breasts, cut into ¾-inch cubes
1 medium onion, diced (1 cup)
½ cup thinly sliced celery (⅛-inch thick)
2 garlic cloves, minced (1 Tbsp.)
½ cup dry white wine (such as pinot grigio)
1 bay leaf
½ tsp. dried thyme
2 large carrots, sliced ¼-inch thick
2 medium russet potatoes, peeled and cut into ½-inch cubes (2 cups)
2½ cups chicken stock (page 12)
salt and pepper to taste
½ cup frozen peas
1 Tbsp. cornstarch mixed with 2 Tbsp. water
double-crust pastry (page 14)
egg wash (1 egg whisked with 1 Tbsp. water)

1 Preheat the oven to 375 degrees F. In a large skillet, fry the bacon until crispy. Transfer the bacon to a paper towel, and pour out all but 1 Tbsp. grease.

2 Add the chicken, and brown on all sides. Add the onions, celery and garlic. Sauté until browned. Add the wine, and scrape up the browned bits from the bottom of the pan. Cook until the wine is reduced by half.

3 Add the bay leaf, thyme, carrots, potato, chicken stock, salt and pepper. Bring to a boil, lower the heat, cover, and simmer for 15 minutes until the vegetables are just tender.

4 Add the reserved bacon and peas. Bring back to a boil, and stir in the cornstarch mixture. Cook for 2 minutes until thickened. Spread onto a sheet pan to cool.

5 Roll out half of the pastry to fit into a deep-dish 10-inch pie plate, and roll out the other half to fit on top. Scrape the chicken filling into the shell, and top with the other half of the pastry. Fold and crimp the edges together, and brush the top with half of the egg wash. Decorate with scrap pastry if desired. Brush with the remaining egg wash. Cut vents in the top crust with a knife or cookie cutter.

6 Bake for 1 hour or until the crust appears golden and the filling bubbles out of the vents. Let rest for 20 minutes before serving.

Duck Pie

Leftover roast duck has never had it so good. The cherries and port make the pie taste a little sweet, the duck enriches the flavor, and a touch of cream brings it all together.

Serves 6

Filling
½ cup dried tart cherries
¼ cup port wine
2 strips thick-cut bacon, cut in ½-inch dice
½ medium onion, diced (½ cup)
6 medium cremini mushrooms, quartered (1 cup)
2 cups duck stock (or chicken stock; see page 12)
3 small sweet potatoes, peeled and cut into ¾-inch cubes (12 oz.)
1 large sprig of fresh thyme
1 bay leaf
salt and pepper to taste
¼ cup heavy cream
1 Tbsp. cornstarch mixed with 2 Tbsp. water
2 cups shredded, cooked duck meat (½ of a 5-lb. roasted duck)

Assembly
double-crust pastry recipe (page 14)
egg wash: 1 egg whisked with 1 Tbsp. water

1 Combine the dried cherries and port in a small bowl. Microwave for 1 minute, and let sit for 20 minutes to rehydrate.

2 In a large sauté pan, fry the bacon until almost crisp. Add the onion and mushrooms, and sauté until softened and starting to brown.

3 Drain the port from the cherries into the pan to deglaze it, scraping up the browned bits on the bottom of the pan. Cook until the wine is reduced to almost nothing.

4 Add the stock, sweet potatoes, thyme, bay leaf, salt and pepper to taste. Simmer for 15 to 20 minutes until the potatoes are tender.

5 Remove and discard the bay leaf. Add the cream and cornstarch mixture. Cook 3 to 4 minutes until the sauce has thickened. Stir in the duck meat and cherries. Spread on a sheet pan to cool.

6 Preheat the oven to 375 degrees F. Roll out half of the pastry, fit it into a 9-inch pie plate, and trim to the edge. Scrape the filling into the crust. Roll out the other half of the pastry, place it on top of the filling, and trim to ½ inch beyond the edge. Tuck the top pastry under the bottom, and crimp to seal the two. Cut vents into the top, and brush with egg wash.

7 Bake for 1 hour. Let rest 20 minutes, and serve.

Chicken Curry Pie with Rice Crust ///////////

This recipe brings a little East-Indian culture. Make it as hot or mild as you like, and substitute any vegetables that you have on hand for the cauliflower or sweet potatoes.

Makes 6 individual servings

Crust
1½ cups chicken stock (page 12)
¾ cup long-grain rice (basmati)
2 Tbsp. minced cilantro
2 eggs, beaten

Filling
1 Tbsp. coconut oil (or butter)
1 medium onion, diced (1 cup)
2 large garlic cloves, minced (1 Tbsp.)
2 Tbsp. minced fresh ginger
2 tsp. curry powder (hot or mild)
1 tsp. brown mustard seeds
1 lb. boneless, skinless chicken breasts or thighs, cut into 1-inch chunks
1½ cups chicken stock (page 12)
1 medium sweet potato, peeled and cut into ½-inch dice (1 cup)
2 cups chopped cauliflower (1-inch pieces)
1 cup diced tomatoes (½-inch pieces — fresh or canned)
3 Tbsp. cornstarch mixed with 3 Tbsp. water
¼ cup coconut milk

1 In a medium pot, bring the chicken stock to a boil. Stir in the rice. Bring back to a boil, lower the heat, cover, and simmer for 15 minutes. Turn off the heat, and let the rice steam for 5 minutes. Let cool. Stir in the cilantro and beaten eggs.

2 In a large sauté pan, melt the coconut oil. Add the onion, garlic and ginger. Sauté until the onion starts to brown. Add the curry powder and mustard seeds, and sauté 1 minute to cook the spices.

3 Add the chicken; brown lightly on all sides. Add the stock, sweet potato, cauliflower and tomatoes. Simmer for 10 to 15 minutes until the vegetables are tender. Stir in the cornstarch mixture and coconut milk. Simmer for 1 to 2 minutes until thickened.

4 Spray 6 1-cup ramekins with nonstick spray. Place ⅓ cup rice mixture in each dish, and press down with a spoon. Divide the chicken mixture among the ramekins, and sprinkle the remaining rice over the chicken — about 2 Tbsp. each. Bake for 30 minutes until the rice starts to brown on top and the filling bubbles. Serve immediately.

TIP

This also can be made in a 9-inch pie plate. Place 2 cups of the rice mixture into the dish, and press onto the bottom and sides. Fill with chicken curry, and sprinkle ½ cup rice on top. Bake for 30 minutes.

TIP Reheat, uncovered, at 350 degrees F for 20 minutes.

Greek Spinach Chicken Pie

This makes a quick meal. You can substitute 2 cups shredded, roast chicken dressed with 2 Tbsp. vinaigrette for the grilled chicken.

Serves 6

Chicken

1 lb. chicken breasts, sliced into ¼-inch-thick strips
¼ cup olive oil
2 Tbsp. lemon juice
1 tsp. dried oregano
½ tsp. salt and pepper

Filling

1 Tbsp. olive oil
2 large garlic cloves, minced (1 Tbsp.)
½ medium onion, diced (½ cup)

10 oz. baby spinach, chopped into 1-inch pieces (6 cups lightly packed)
4 oz. crumbled feta cheese
1 cup ricotta cheese
1 egg, lightly beaten
salt and pepper to taste
1 tsp. lemon zest

Assembly

¼ cup olive oil
14 sheets phyllo dough (half of a package with a few left over)

1 In a bowl, combine the chicken with the oil, lemon juice, oregano, salt and pepper. Marinate in the refrigerator for 1 hour. Heat a grill pan or outdoor grill to high. Grill the chicken strips about 3 minutes per side until just tender.

2 In a large skillet, heat the oil. Add the garlic and onion, and sauté until softened. Add the spinach, and toss frequently until completely wilted. Use a paper towel to dab excess liquid. Transfer to a medium bowl, and stir in the feta cheese, ricotta, egg, salt, pepper and lemon zest.

3 Preheat the oven to 400 degrees F. Use 6 sheets of phyllo dough for the bottom crust and 8 for the top. Carefully unroll the dough, and keep a clean, damp towel over the top so it doesn't dry out.

4 Place 1 sheet on your work surface, and brush lightly with olive oil. Lay the next sheet of phyllo perpendicular on the first one, and brush with oil. Continue layering and brushing the layers, placing the next one to fill in the spaces so you end up with a somewhat round stack of pastries, each with oil in between.

5 Ease into a 9-inch pie plate, and roll the edges toward the center until you reach the rim of the pan. Spread with half of the spinach-cheese mixture. Place all of the chicken in a single layer. Finish with the remaining cheese, spreading it to cover the chicken.

6 Brush each of the remaining 8 sheets of phyllo dough with olive oil, and scrunch each one loosely into a ball. Place on top of the filling with one in the center and the others encircling it.

7 Bake for 30 minutes — until the pastry is golden-brown and crispy and the filling bubbles. Let rest 10 to 15 minutes before serving.

Meaty Pies

RECIPES AND PHOTOS BY PATRICIA LEHNHARDT

pies made with beef, ham and pork make hearty, tasty meals.

Shepherd's Pie

This dish offers a quick fix for a comforting, meat-and-potatoes meal. Make the meat mixture in larger quantities, and freeze it in portion sizes. You'll need only mashed potatoes and 30 minutes in the oven for a hearty meal on the table.

Serves 6

1 lb. ground lamb
2 garlic cloves, minced (1 Tbsp.)
2 carrots, peeled and diced into ¼-inch pieces
   (1 cup)
½ tsp. dried thyme
2 tsp. Worcestershire sauce
1½ cups beef stock (page 13)
2 Tbsp. tomato paste
½ cup frozen peas
1 cup frozen pearl onions
salt and pepper to taste

Topping
3 large russet potatoes, peeled and cubed (about
   2 lbs.)
3 Tbsp. butter
½ cup buttermilk
salt and pepper to taste
pinch of paprika

1 Brown the meat in a large skillet, breaking it up with a spatula as it cooks. Add the garlic, carrots, thyme, Worcestershire sauce, beef stock and tomato paste. Simmer for 15 minutes until the carrots are tender. Add 2 Tbsp. stock if needed to prevent the mixture from drying out.

2 Stir in the peas and onions, and cook 1 minute until defrosted. Add salt and pepper to taste. Pour the mixture into a 1½-quart casserole dish or 6 individual dishes (1 cup in each).

3 Preheat the oven to 400 degrees Fahrenheit. Place the potatoes in a medium saucepan, and cover with water. Cover the pan, bring to a boil, lower the heat, and simmer until the potatoes are just tender — about 10 to 15 minutes. Drain the pan, and mash the potatoes with the butter, buttermilk, salt and pepper. Cool for 10 minutes.

4 Transfer to a pastry bag, and pipe onto the top of the meat pie. Sprinkle with paprika.

5 Bake for 30 minutes. Turn the oven to broil, and bake until the tips of the potatoes look golden-brown — about 5 minutes. Serve the pie immediately.

Beef Bourguignon Pie

This is a classic French stew made into a mixed-pastry pie in true French fashion. Fresh thyme and red wine add to the earthiness of the beef to create true comfort.

Serves 6

Filling
2 slices thick-cut bacon, cut into ½-inch dice
1 lb. sirloin steak, cut into ¾-inch cubes
salt and pepper to taste
2 Tbsp. all-purpose flour
1 cup dry red wine (such as cabernet sauvignon)
2 Tbsp. tomato paste
1½ cups beef stock (page 13)
1½ tsp. fresh thyme
2 bay leaves
1 cup frozen pearl onions, thawed
3 carrots, cut into 1½-inch chunks
6 medium cremini mushrooms, quartered
2 Tbsp. melted butter
2 Tbsp. all-purpose flour

1 single-crust pastry, blind baked in a 9-inch pie plate (page 14)

Biscuits
1 cup flour
¼ tsp. baking soda
¾ tsp. baking powder
½ tsp. salt
1 tsp. fresh thyme
4 Tbsp. butter
6 Tbsp. buttermilk

1 Fry the bacon in a large sauté pan until crisp. Remove the bacon, and drain on paper towels. Drain all but 1 Tbsp. grease, reserving the grease in the pan to use later.

2 On a plate, toss the beef with the salt, pepper and flour.

3 Add the beef to the pan, and cook until brown on all sides. Add the red wine and tomato paste. Scrape up all of the browned bits on the bottom of the pan, and simmer for 10 minutes. Add the beef stock, thyme and bay leaves. Cover, and

simmer for 30 to 40 minutes until the meat becomes tender.

4 Meanwhile, heat 1 Tbsp. bacon grease in a small skillet. Add the onions, carrots and mushrooms, and sauté until brown. Add to the beef stew, and simmer 15 minutes until the carrots become tender. Remove the bay leaves, and stir in the reserved bacon bits.

5 In a separate bowl, mix the melted butter and flour, and whisk into the stew. Simmer for 5 minutes until thickened. Preheat the oven to 425 degrees F.

6 Make the biscuit dough while the stew simmers and the bottom crust bakes (see below). In a medium bowl, mix the flour, baking soda, baking powder, salt and thyme. Cut in the butter until it resembles old-fashioned oat flakes. Stir in the buttermilk until the dough comes together. Knead a couple of times to incorporate all of the flour.

7 Roll the biscuit dough to ¼-inch thickness, and use a small cutter to cut out as many 1-inch disks as you can.

8 Pour the beef stew into the prebaked crust, and top with the biscuits. Bake for 20 minutes until the biscuits appear golden and the filling bubbles. Serve immediately.

Blind Bake the Bottom Crust

1 Preheat the oven to 425 degrees F.

2 Roll out the pastry, and ease into a 9-inch pie plate. Trim the edges, fold under, and crimp. Place a sheet of parchment paper into the crust, and fill with dried beans or pie weights. Bake for 15 minutes. Remove the parchment and beans.

Ham and Broccoli
Pot Pie with Cheddar Topper

This recipe takes the popular creamy soup and turns it into a pie with Cheddar cheese pastry.

Serves 6

Crust
1 cup all-purpose flour
½ cup grated Cheddar cheese
¼ tsp. salt
⅛ tsp. freshly ground pepper
⅛ tsp. chipotle chili powder
¼ cup butter, chilled
2 Tbsp. organic vegetable shortening
1 Tbsp. vodka
4 Tbsp. water
3 ice cubes

Filling
3 Tbsp. butter
1 medium onion, diced (1 cup)
1 small red bell pepper, diced (1 cup)
6 medium cremini mushrooms, diced (1 cup)
¼ cup all-purpose flour
2 cups milk
1 Tbsp. spicy brown mustard
dash of hot sauce to taste (such as Tabasco)
1 cup shredded Cheddar cheese
3 cups steamed broccoli florets
12 oz. smoked ham, cut into ½-inch cubes

Egg wash: 1 egg beaten with 1 Tbsp. water

1 In a large, shallow bowl, combine the flour, cheese, salt, pepper and chipotle powder. Using the large holes on a box grater, shred the butter into the flour, fluffing it with your fingers so the flour coats the butter without forming large clumps.

2 Pinch the shortening into small bits, and toss into the flour. With both hands, lightly rub the mixture to even out the texture.

3 In a small cup, combine the vodka and water, and add ice cubes. Drizzle the liquid into the flour, holding back the ice. With your fingers, work the dough until it forms a mass. Do not overwork the dough. Press gently into a disk, wrap in plastic, and refrigerate for 30 minutes.

4 While the dough chills, make the filling. Melt the butter in a large sauté pan. Add the onion, bell pepper and mushrooms. Sauté until softened and starting to brown.

5 Preheat the oven to 400 degrees F. Stir in the flour. Cook for 1 minute, stirring to cook the raw taste from the flour. Add the milk, and stir to create the sauce. Simmer for 5 minutes. Remove from the heat, and stir in the mustard, hot sauce, cheese, broccoli and ham. Mix.

6 Pour the ham mixture into a 1½-quart casserole dish. Roll out the pastry to fit the dish. Place the dough on top of the meat mixture, and press the pastry to the edges of the dish. Tear off the excess pastry to create a ragged look, or trim neatly and crimp. Brush with egg wash, and cut vents in the top. Bake for 30 minutes until the pastry becomes golden and the filling bubbles out of the vents. Serve immediately.

Italian Sausage and Potato Pie with Parmesan Drop Biscuits

This recipe features all of the elements of a great Italian meal in one dish. For a quick dinner, make the filling in the morning and the biscuits when you get home from work. Bake the filling alone for 10 minutes before adding the biscuit dough to give it a head-start after re-frigeration.

Serves 6

1 lb. Italian pork sausage, mild or hot
1 medium onion, diced (1 cup)
1 small red bell pepper, diced (1 cup)
3 large cremini mushrooms, cut into ½-inch chunks
2 garlic cloves, minced
salt and pepper to taste
1 tsp. Italian seasoning
½ cup dry red wine (such as cabernet sauvignon)
1 cup beef stock (page 13)
3 medium russet potatoes, peeled and cut into ½-inch dice
1½ cups diced tomatoes (fresh or canned)
1 Tbsp. cornstarch mixed with 2 Tbsp. water

Parmesan biscuits
1 cup all-purpose flour
½ cup finely grated Parmesan cheese plus 2 Tbsp. for topping
1 tsp. finely minced fresh rosemary
2 tsp. baking powder
½ tsp. baking soda
2 Tbsp. butter, chilled
¾ cup buttermilk

1 In a large skillet, fry the sausage until it starts to brown, breaking it up with a spatula as it cooks. Drain any excess grease, leaving about 1 Tbsp. in the pan. Add the onion, bell pepper, mushrooms, garlic, salt, pepper and Italian seasoning. Sauté until the vegetables are tender and start to brown on the bottom.

2 Add the wine, and cook down until it no longer remains visible, scraping up the brown bits in the bottom of the pan. Add the beef stock, potatoes and tomatoes. Cover the pan, bring to a boil, lower the heat, and simmer for 10 minutes or until the potatoes are just tender. Stir in the corn-starch mixture, and cook 1 minute, stirring until the gravy has thickened. Pour into a 1½-quart casserole dish.

3 Preheat the oven to 425 degrees F. In a medium bowl, combine the flour, ½ cup Parmesan cheese, rosemary, baking powder and baking soda. Grate the butter into the mixture using a large-holed grater. Fluff the butter so that each strand be-comes coated with flour. Stir in the buttermilk just until incorporated.

4 Drop 6 biscuits on the top of the stew, and sprinkle with the remaining 2 Tbsp. Parmesan. Bake for 20 minutes. Serve immediately.

Philly Cheese Steak Pies with Caramelized Onions and Provolone Sauce

///

Assembled individual pies are presented here. It's easy to make all of the components ahead of time and fry the steak at the last minute; then dinner or lunch is on the table quickly. When made even smaller, these offer great, hearty party fare.

Makes 6 individual pies

single-crust pastry recipe (page 14)

Egg wash: 1 egg beaten with 1 Tbsp. water
1 tsp. sesame seeds

Caramelized onions
1 large onion, thinly sliced
1 Tbsp. olive oil
salt and pepper to taste

Steak
12 oz. rib-eye steak, trimmed
½ tsp. salt

¼ tsp. freshly ground pepper
½ tsp. smoked paprika
½ tsp. dried oregano
2 tsp. olive oil

Cheese sauce
2 Tbsp. butter
1 Tbsp. flour
1 cup milk
4 oz. shredded smoked Provolone cheese

Mushrooms and green pepper
4 medium cremini mushrooms, thinly sliced
1 small green bell pepper, sliced ¼-inch thick
2 tsp. olive oil

Assembly
1 Tbsp. chopped parsley

1 Preheat the oven to 425 degrees F. Roll out the dough to less than ⅛-inch thickness. Cut out

6 rounds to fit into 4-inch tart pans. Also cut out 6 2½-inch rounds for the tops. Fit the larger rounds into the pans or drape them over 4-oz. ramekins to form the tarts.

2 Place the smaller rounds on a small baking sheet. Brush with the egg wash, and sprinkle sesame seeds on the small toppers. Refrigerate for 30 minutes. Bake for 15 minutes until golden. Remove, and cool on a rack.

3 In a medium skillet, combine the onion, oil, salt and pepper. Sauté, stirring occasionally, over medium-low heat until the onions become very soft and golden-brown — about 20 to 30 minutes.

4 Place the steak in the freezer for 30 minutes to firm. Slice as thinly as you can.

5 Mix the salt, pepper, paprika and oregano in a small bowl. Sprinkle evenly over the meat; mix.

6 Heat the oil on high heat in a large, heavy skillet until hot and shimmering. Add the meat, and cook quickly, stirring so it browns on all sides with a few pink spots — approximately 3 to 4 minutes.

7 Melt the butter in a small pot, and whisk in the flour. Cook for 1 to 2 minutes, whisking occasionally. Whisk in the milk, and cook until thickened. Take off the heat, and stir in the cheese until melted.

8 In a separate pan, sauté the mushrooms and pepper in the oil until browned and tender.

9 When all of the components are ready, assemble your pies: bottom tart crust, a portion of steak, onions, mushrooms and peppers. Dollop on a spoonful of the cheese sauce, sprinkle with parsley, and top with a sesame-seed pastry. Serve immediately.

Reuben Pie

All the elements of a Reuben sandwich are baked into a pie. If you reheat uncovered at 350 degrees F for 30 minutes, the cheese will become ooey-gooey once again.

Serves 6

Rye crust
1½ cups all-purpose flour
½ cup dark rye flour
½ tsp. salt
1 tsp. ground caraway seed (grind whole caraway seeds in a small electric coffee grinder)
½ cup butter, chilled
¼ cup organic vegetable shortening
3 Tbsp. vodka
6 Tbsp. water
3 to 4 ice cubes

Filling
2 Tbsp. butter
1 medium onion, sliced (1 cup)
3 cups thinly sliced cabbage
1 large russet potato, peeled and thinly sliced (about 2 cups)
salt and pepper to taste
1 Tbsp. apple cider vinegar
½ cup heavy cream
2½ cups cubed (½ inch), cooked corned beef
4 oz. shredded Swiss cheese

Egg wash: 1 egg beaten with 1 Tbsp. water

1 In a large, shallow bowl, combine the flours, salt and caraway. Grate in the butter using a large-holed grater. Fluff the butter shreds with the flour so each becomes coated with flour.

2 Pinch off tiny bits of shortening, and add to the mix. Using your hands, gently rub the mixture to even out the texture and break up clumps of fat that might have formed.

3 Mix the vodka and water in a glass, and add a few ice cubes. Drizzle in the iced liquid a little at a time, mixing it into the flour with your hands. Continue until all of the water appears incorporated. Knead a couple of times in the bowl until the dough comes together.

4 Divide the dough in half, flatten each portion into a disk, and wrap in plastic. Refrigerate for 30 minutes.

5 Melt the butter in a large sauté pan. Add the onion, cabbage, potato, salt and pepper. Cover, and cook over low heat, turning occasionally, until all of the vegetables become tender — about 20 minutes. You might need to add a bit of water if the mixture becomes too dry.

6 Stir in the vinegar, cream and corned beef. Spread out on a sheet pan to cool.

7 Preheat the oven to 375 degrees. F. Roll out half of the dough into a disk about 12 inches in diameter. Place it on a 9-inch pie plate, and ease into the sides. Trim to the outer edge of the pie plate.

8 Scrape the filling into the pie dough, and top with the Swiss cheese. Roll out the other half of the dough. Place on top of the filling. Trim to ½ inch beyond the edge, tuck under the bottom crust,

and crimp the two together to seal. Cut vents in the dough, and brush with half of the egg wash. Decorate with pastry scraps, cut into shapes if desired, and brush again with the remaining egg wash.

9 Bake for 1 hour until the crust appears golden and the filling bubbles through the vents. Rest for 20 minutes before serving.

Veggie Pot Pies

RECIPES BY SAMANTHA JOHNSON
AND PAULETTE JOHNSON
PHOTOS BY DANIEL JOHNSON

when you think of a pot pie, do you automatically think of a dish that features chicken, turkey or beef? Don't let those preconceived stereotypes limit your pot-pie experience! Vegetarian pot pies offer the perfect vehicle for showcasing the hearty flavors of sometimes-overlooked nonmeat ingredients. Explore an array of vegetables, cheeses and other edibles as you acquaint yourself with six vegetarian pot pies. What are you waiting for? A world of pot-pie wonder awaits!

BrocCauli-Cheddar Pot Pie

Warm, creamy, and delicious — perfect for a cold afternoon! This pot pie combines the top-notch trio of broccoli, cheese and cauliflower into a jam-packed cheesy-veggie sensation. Whip up this pot pie for a tummy-pleasing lunch, and enjoy the flavorful fun.

Makes 1 9-inch pot pie

1 cup cream
2 Tbsp. flour
8 oz. sharp Cheddar, grated
1 tsp. onion powder
½ tsp. salt
½ tsp. pepper
1½ cups broccoli, steamed and chopped (fresh or frozen)
1½ cups cauliflower, steamed and chopped (fresh or frozen)
double-crust recipe (page 14; enough for a 9-inch pie pan)

1 In a saucepan over medium heat, combine the cream and flour. Whisk constantly until it boils. Reduce the heat to medium-low, and continue whisking until the sauce thickens. Watch closely to prevent burning.

2 Once the sauce has thickened, gradually add the Cheddar ¼ cup at a time. Stir the cheese until thoroughly melted; then add the onion powder, salt and pepper. Remove from heat.

3 Add the broccoli and cauliflower in ½-cup increments, and stir until coated.

4 Preheat the oven to 375 degrees Fahrenheit. Prepare the pie crust dough according to the recipe on page 14. Place one pie crust in the bottom of a 9-inch pie pan. Pour the vegetable-cheese mixture into the pan. Place the second pie crust on top; crimp the edges. If desired, add an egg wash (1 egg whisked with 1 Tbsp. water or milk) to the top of the crust. Cut a few slits in the top to let the steam escape.

5 Bake for 35 to 45 minutes or until the crust becomes golden-brown.

Rise 'n Shine Pot Pie

Looking for the perfect way to start your day? This unbelievable breakfast pot pie sets the tone for a delightful and delicious day. You can serve it as an ultra-tasty lunch or dinner, too. This dish combines favorite breakfast necessities — hash browns, eggs and toast — into one stick-to-your-ribs pot pie.

Makes 3 to 4 servings

4 cups hash browns, prepared (you can add onions and peppers if desired)
4 oz. grated Swiss cheese
5 eggs
½ tsp. salt
½ tsp. pepper
½ tsp. onion powder
2 Tbsp. cream cheese
3 Tbsp. butter
4 bread slices with the crusts removed

1 Preheat the oven to 350 degrees F. Place the hash browns in a greased 6-by-9-inch baking dish. Add the Swiss cheese over the hash browns.

2 In a bowl, whisk together the eggs, salt, pepper and onion powder; then transfer to a large skillet.

3 Cook over medium-low heat, adding the cream cheese as the eggs cook. Remove from heat when the eggs are cooked through but still soft and moist. Pour the eggs over the cheese/hash brown mixture.

4 In a saucepan over low heat, melt the butter; then remove from heat. Lightly butter both sides of each slice of bread; then place the slices on top of the egg/cheese/hash brown mixture.

5 Bake for 20 minutes or until the bread is toasted.

Everything-but-the-Chicken Pot Pie

Who needs chicken when you can throw together a simple pot pie that's jam-packed with savory goodness? This super-easy cast-iron sensation combines truckloads of veggies with a palate-pleasing blend of spices. By using frozen vegetables, you can literally put this dish together in minutes. Use whatever you have in the freezer that looks yummy. You really can't put in too much or too little! Top everything off with mouthwatering biscuits, and you have all of the components for a splendiferous meal.

Makes 10 to 12 servings

2 medium onions, chopped
3 Tbsp. butter
1 16-oz. bag of frozen, mixed vegetables
1 14- to 16-oz. bag of frozen peas
1 8-ounce bag of frozen corn
2¼ cups water or vegetable stock (page 10)
¼ tsp. dried parsley
⅛ tsp. turmeric
½ tsp. salt
⅛ tsp. celery seed
⅛ tsp. pepper
1 tsp. garlic powder
1 cup cream
1 cup milk
½ cup flour
12 3-inch biscuits, unbaked (you can use refrigerated biscuit dough or make your own)

1 Preheat the oven to 375 degrees F. In a 15-inch cast iron skillet over medium heat, sauté the onions in the butter until soft.

2 Add the vegetables and the water or stock, and continue stirring. Add the parsley, turmeric, salt, celery seed, pepper and garlic powder, and continue stirring. Add the cream and milk, stirring frequently.

3 In small amounts, gradually add the flour over the top of the vegetables. The sauce will thicken. Add additional flour or liquid in 1 Tbsp. increments as needed to achieve the desired creaminess.

4 Arrange the unbaked biscuits over the top of the vegetable mixture. Bake for 20 minutes or until golden-brown.

Stuffin' and Peppers Pot Pie

Celebrate the joy of Thanksgiving at any time of the year! This pot pie features soothingly satisfying stuffing and plenty of colorful peppers, topped off with fluffy mashed potatoes. It's a steamy, creamy, dreamy experience that will leave guests begging for more.

Makes 4 servings

3 cups stuffing, prepared as desired
1 cup corn, cooked
1 yellow bell pepper, chopped
1 green bell pepper, chopped
1 red bell pepper, chopped
1 medium onion, chopped
1 tsp. salt
½ tsp. pepper
2 Tbsp. dried parsley, divided
1 cup water
3 cups of mashed potatoes, prepared as desired
⅓ cup mozzarella, grated

1 Preheat the oven to 375 degrees F. Distribute the prepared stuffing evenly among 4 4-inch ramekins.

2 In a large skillet, place the corn, peppers, onion, salt, pepper, 1 Tbsp. parsley and water. Cook over medium heat until the vegetables become soft.

3 Transfer the vegetable mixture to the ramekins, and distribute on top of the stuffing. (Include the liquid from the skillet.)

4 Mix the potatoes with the remaining 1 Tbsp. of parsley, and transfer to the ramekins, placing the potatoes on top of the vegetables. Sprinkle the tops with mozzarella.

5 Bake for 20 to 25 minutes or until the potatoes begin to turn golden.

Sweet Potato Crunch Pot Pie ///////////////////////////////

Sweet potatoes star in this stunning dish, and their gorgeous coloring only accentuates the sweetly spicy taste. With a satisfying bit of crunch in the form of the marshmallow-infused cereal topping, this pot pie makes a sure-fire winner.

Makes 6 to 8 servings

4 medium sweet potatoes, peeled and chopped into
   ¾-inch chunks
⅛ tsp. ginger
⅛ tsp. cayenne pepper
½ tsp. cinnamon
¼ cup maple syrup
1 cup cream
3 Tbsp. butter
20 to 22 large marshmallows
3 cups cinnamon rice cereal, crushed to crumbs

1 Preheat the oven to 375 degrees F. In a saucepan, boil the sweet potatoes until fork-tender — about 15 to 20 minutes. Drain the water.

2 In the same saucepan over low heat, add the ginger, cayenne pepper, cinnamon, maple syrup and cream. Stir until the sweet potatoes are coated.

3 Grease a 9-inch pie pan, and pour the sweet potatoes into it.

4 In a saucepan, heat the butter; then add the marshmallows. Slowly melt the marshmallows; then remove from heat, and quickly add the crushed cereal.

5 Place the marshmallow-cereal mixture between two sheets of wax paper, and roll it out until flattened.

6 Break the cereal into pieces, and arrange the pieces over the potatoes. (This makes the pie easier to cut through later.)

7 Bake for 20 minutes.

Five-cheese Pizza Pot Pie

What's better than a super-cheesy pizza topped with all of your favorite veggies? We think this pizza-inspired pot pie gives the original a real run for its money. Give it a try with whatever "toppings" you desire. This pizza pot pie is all about excess — and this recipe makes enough to serve a party!

Makes 12 to 14 servings

Filling
3 cups pizza sauce (use your favorite)
2 Tbsp. butter
1 red pepper, chopped
1 yellow pepper, chopped
2 green peppers, chopped
2 medium onions, chopped
¾ cup mushrooms, sliced (optional)
4 oz. grated Swiss cheese
8 oz. grated Monterey Jack cheese
8 oz. grated sharp Cheddar
8 oz. grated mozzarella

Crust
2 cups warm water (110 to 115 degrees F)
2 packets (¼ oz. each) active-dry yeast
1 tsp. sugar, divided
5 cups flour
2 Tbsp. vegetable oil
1 cup Parmesan cheese
2 Tbsp. dried parsley

1. Place the pizza sauce in a lightly greased 11-by-15-inch baking dish.

2. In a large skillet over medium-high heat, melt the butter, and sauté the vegetables until they begin to soften. Remove from the heat, and set aside.

3. Layer the Swiss, Monterey Jack, Cheddar and mozzarella cheeses over the sauce. Add the sautéed vegetables on top of the cheese.

4. Add a packet of yeast to ¼ cup of very warm water. Add ½ tsp. sugar, and set aside until it foams and bubbles (about 5 to 10 minutes).

5. Preheat the oven to 425 degrees F. In a large mixing bowl, combine the flour, remaining water, yeast mixture, remaining sugar, vegetable oil, Parmesan cheese and parsley. Stir until it forms dough. Set aside to rise for 30 minutes.

6. Knead the dough for approximately 5 minutes; then roll it out to fit the 11-by-15-inch pan. Place the crust on top of the other ingredients in the pan, and adjust it to fit, rolling up the edges as necessary. You don't want the crust to hang over the edge of the pan.

7. Bake for 25 to 30 minutes until the crust looks golden.

Seafood Pies

RECIPES AND PHOTOS BY PATRICIA LEHNHARDT

Give your pies a splash of the ocean.

Lobster Pot Pie for Two

This makes a decadent dinner that's perfect for an intimate celebration — or whenever you want to enjoy the rich, sweet flavor of lobster dressed up with mushrooms, wine and cream.

Serves 2

Quick puff pastry (small portion)
¾ cup all-purpose flour
⅛ tsp. salt
6 Tbsp. butter, cut into ¼-inch cubes
3 Tbsp. ice water

Filling
2 small lobster tails (about 1 lb. total)
2 Tbsp. butter, divided
⅓ cup diced onion
⅓ cup thinly sliced celery
⅓ cup diced red bell pepper
3 medium cremini mushrooms, diced
1 carrot, cut into ¼-by-2-inch pieces
¼ cup dry white wine
1 cup heavy cream
½ tsp. fresh thyme leaves
salt and freshly ground pepper to taste
⅓ cup frozen peas
1 egg whisked with 1 Tbsp. water

1 Prepare the puff pastry: In a medium bowl, mix the flour and salt, and add the butter. Using your fingers and/or a pastry cutter, cut and smash the butter into smaller pieces. Incorporate the flour until you see only a few large pieces the size of dried beans.

2 Sprinkle the water over the flour-and-butter mixture, and use your finger to help the dough come together. It will form a rough mass.

3 Press into a rectangle on a floured surface. Use a rolling pin, and roll out to ¼-inch thick. Fold the pastry in thirds with the help of a bench scraper, folding one-third of the dough into the center and the other end over the top like a letter.

4 Turn the dough, and reroll it, folding and turning five or six times.

It should form a cohesive, smooth pastry dough. Wrap in plastic, and refrigerate for 30 minutes.

5 Preheat the oven to 350 degrees Fahrenheit. Now, make the filling. Split the lobster tails in half, and arrange them cut-side up in a small roasting pan. Spread 1 Tbsp. butter on top. Bake for 15 to 20 minutes until no longer translucent. Remove the meat from the shells, and cut into 1-inch chunks.

6 Increase the temperature of the oven to 425 degrees F. In a medium frying pan, melt the remaining butter. Add the onion, celery, bell pepper, mushrooms and carrot. Sauté until the vegetables start to brown — about 5 minutes.

7 Add the white wine, and scrape up any browned bits from the bottom of the pan. Let the wine cook until reduced. You should have about 2 Tbsp. left in the pan.

8 Add the cream, thyme, salt and pepper, and cook on high to reduce the cream by half. The vegetables should all be tender by now. Stir in the lobster and peas, and divide the mixture between two small, round casserole dishes (1½-cup capacity).

9 Roll out the puff pastry, and cut to fit the tops of your dishes. Brush with half of the egg wash, decorate with pastry scraps, if desired, and brush with egg again.

10 Bake for 20 minutes — until the pastry looks puffed and golden and the lobster mixture bubbles up the sides. Serve immediately.

Salmon Pie

This seafood pie is loosely based on Russian coulibiac. With flaky pastry enclosing salmon and rice in a lemony sauce, it is perfect for a holiday party or any celebration.

Serves 8 to 9

Filling
12 oz. salmon filet
1 tsp. olive oil
salt and pepper to taste

Rice
1 Tbsp. butter
½ cup finely chopped onion
½ cup long-grained white rice (basmati)
1 cup water
½ tsp. salt

Mushrooms
1 Tbsp. butter
1 large shallot, minced
6 medium (1½ cups lightly packed) cremini
    mushrooms, finely minced
¼ tsp. dried thyme
salt and pepper to taste
2 Tbsp. brandy

Sauce
½ cup white wine
1 cup clam juice
2 Tbsp. lemon juice
1 Tbsp. cornstarch dissolved in 2 Tbsp. water
3 Tbsp. butter
1 Tbsp. fresh dill weed, chopped
salt and pepper to taste

Assembly
all-purpose double crust (page 14)
1 egg whisked with 1 Tbsp. water

1 Preheat the oven to 450 degrees F. Place the salmon on a baking sheet, brush with olive oil, and season with salt and pepper. Bake for 8 minutes. Cool, and flake.

2 In a small pot, melt the butter. Add the onion, and sauté until softened and starting to brown. Add the rice, and sauté 1 minute, stirring to coat the rice with butter.

3 Add water and salt. Bring to a boil, lower the heat, cover, and simmer for about 15 minutes. Remove from heat, and rest for at least 5 minutes.

4 To prepare the mushrooms, melt the butter in a medium skillet. Add the shallot and mushrooms. Cook until the mushrooms have released all of their liquid and started to brown. Add the thyme, salt, pepper and brandy. Cook 1 minute.

5 Now, make the sauce. Pour the wine into a small pot, and cook over high heat until reduced by half. Add the clam juice and lemon

juice. Simmer for 5 minutes. Whisk in the corn-starch mixture, butter, dill, salt and pepper. Cook for 1 minute, whisking until thickened. Set aside to cool.

6 Preheat the oven to 375 degrees F. Roll out the bottom crust, and ease into an 8-by-8-inch glass baking pan. Layer the ingredients into the pie shell in the following order: half of the rice, half of the salmon, all of the mushrooms, the rest of the

rice and the rest of the salmon. Pour the sauce evenly over the filling.

7 Cover with the top crust, and crimp the edges. Cut vents into the top crust, and paint with egg wash. (Weave the crust as seen above if desired.)

8 Bake 1 hour until the crust appears golden and the filling bubbles out of the vents. Rest for 20 minutes before serving.

Slow-cooker Recipes

RECIPES AND PHOTOS BY RHODA PEACHER

you can use a slow cooker to ease the pie-making process.

Slow-cooker Beef Pot Pie

Traditional pot-pie crust can't be made in a slow cooker. This beef recipe is based on shepherd's pie and topped with mashed potatoes.

Serves 6 to 8

3½ to 4 lbs. beef chuck roast
salt and pepper to taste
3 Tbsp. vegetable oil
2 medium onions, chopped
⅓ cup flour
1½ to 2 cups low-sodium chicken stock, divided
2 dashes Worcestershire sauce
⅛ tsp. ground allspice
1 bay leaf
5 carrots, cut into ¼-inch-thick rounds
3 cups mashed potatoes (use your favorite recipe)

1 Sprinkle the beef with salt and pepper. In a large pot, heat the oil until shimmering but not smoking. Brown the meat on all sides — about 6 to 8 minutes per side. Remove the meat from the pot, and set aside.

2 Using the same pot, sauté the onions until translucent. Add the flour and cook, stirring continuously until the flour becomes toasted without burning. Whisk in 1 cup chicken stock, and cook until slightly thickened. Add the Worcestershire sauce, allspice, bay leaf and carrots, and mix.

3 Put the meat in a slow cooker. If it's a thick cut, you can cut it in half horizontally so it sits lower in the pot and covers more of the bottom. Pour the onion and chicken-stock mixture over the meat, and add more stock if needed to cover the meat. Cover, and cook on the low setting for 7 to 8 hours.

4 When the meat is done, remove it from the cooker. Let the cooking liquid sit for 10 minutes so the fat rises to the surface and you can skim it off. While waiting, pull the meat apart into 1-inch chunks, return to the cooker, and stir. Spread the mashed potatoes on top of the meat and liquid, and serve.

Tomatillo Chicken Pot Pie

This chicken pot pie features a cornbread topping instead of a traditional pastry crust. The cornbread provides a good accompaniment to the spicy Southwest flavors in the tomatillo salsa.

Serves 4

2 lbs. boneless skinless chicken thighs
salt and pepper to taste
3 cups of your favorite tomatillo salsa (I recommend the recipe in Altrista Consumer Products' "Ball Blue Book Guide to Preserving," but a storebought salsa will work.)
1½ Tbsp. instant tapioca pearls
3 to 4 cups of your favorite cornbread batter [I used the "crackling cornbread" recipe from "Joy of Cooking" by Irma S. Rombauer, Marion Rombauer Becker and Ethan Becker (Scribner), but any recipe or mix would be fine.]

1 Cut the chicken into 1½-inch pieces, and sprinkle with salt and pepper to taste.

2 Place the chicken in the slow cooker, and cover with tomatillo salsa. Stir in the tapioca.

3 Gently spread the cornbread batter over the top of the chicken without mixing it in. Cover, and cook on low for 5 hours before serving.

Vegan Pot Pies

RECIPES AND PHOTOS BY KYRA KIRKWOOD

vegan ingredients add health and flavor to pot-pie recipes.

Creamy Cashew Winter Harvest

Nothing says "comfort food" like a piping-hot pot pie. This creamy, fragrant, slightly nutty dish blends the caramelized taste of root vegetables like sweet potatoes with the crisp crunch of fennel and green beans. The apple bakes up wonderfully and adds just a hint of candied goodness to the whole mix. It's like a warm winter's embrace all wrapped up in a buttery-tasting blanket of whole-wheat crust. This pot pie is so hearty and delicious that even your meat-eating friends might ask for seconds.

Note: Unless stated, you do not need to chop or slice the vegetables into one precise size, but make sure the pieces are all bite-sized. Also, use fresh produce — and organic if at all possible.

Makes 4 large servings and 6 regular ones

2 cups raw cashews
2 Tbsp. olive oil
2 garlic cloves, finely chopped
½ large yellow onion, finely chopped
1 large carrot, sliced
1 medium sweet potato, peeled and chopped (about 1¼ cups)
2 celery stalks, chopped
½ cup mushrooms, sliced
½ fennel bulb, sliced and chopped
1 medium apple (a crisp one like Granny Smith), cored and chopped (no need to peel)
¾ cup green beans, cut
½ medium red bell pepper, chopped
⅔ cup chickpeas, drained and rinsed
¼ tsp. marjoram
¼ tsp. dried basil
¼ tsp. dried ginger
¼ tsp. paprika
a scant sprinkle of cayenne pepper (optional)
1 cup vegetable broth
1½ Tbsp. soy sauce
1 Tbsp. apple cider vinegar
a few dashes of black pepper (to taste)
pinch of salt (to taste)

Crust
½ cup all-purpose white flour
½ cup whole-wheat flour
1 tsp. salt
⅓ cup vegan "butter," very cold
4 to 6 Tbsp. ice water

1 Preheat the oven to 350 degrees Fahrenheit. Soak the cashews in a large bowl filled with very hot water (you can use the hottest setting on your kitchen

faucet). Let them sit while you prepare the rest of the dish. You also can do this step early, letting the nuts soak for 4 hours or longer.

2 Heat the olive oil in a very large skillet or wok over medium-high heat. Add the garlic and onions; then add the rest of the vegetables except for the beans, peppers and chickpeas. Cook for about 5 minutes; then add the apple, beans, peppers, chickpeas and spices. Stir to combine, and continue to cook until the potatoes and apple become slightly tender and the rest of the vegetables are gently browned and cooked through. Turn off the heat.

3 Next, drain the cashews and place them in a blender with the broth, soy sauce and apple cider vinegar. Blend from low to high until completely smooth and creamy. This can take 1 minute or longer, depending on your blender.

4 Pour the entire mixture over the vegetables. Turn the heat on the stove to medium-high, and stir everything together. Cook until the vegetables and sauce are well-combined and a nutty flavor begins to develop. This takes about 2 minutes. Season with salt and pepper to taste.

5 Pour everything into your baking dish. I've used a 9-by-12-inch dish; any similar vessel will work well. If you choose to make the pot pie in individual ramekins, portion the dough by rolling it out and cutting out shapes to cover the tops of the pies. You might need to cut and roll numerous times.

6 For the crust, mix the two flours along with the salt in a large bowl. Add the buttery spread, and cut it into the flour using a butter knife or pastry cutter. Mix in the water 1 Tbsp. at a time until the mixture forms a ball. Knead with your hands, and place on a floured surface.

7 Roll thin (about ¼- to ⅛-inch thick), and place over the vegetable-filled baking dish. Pinch the sides to form an edge, and cut a small slit in the middle. Bake for 35 minutes. Cool for 5 minutes; then serve.

*Note: This recipe makes a lot of sauce, so add more vegetables if you desire. This can cut down on the calorie count and bump up the fiber, too. Just make sure everything fits into your dish and is covered by the crust.

Savory Pot Pie with Tofu and Potatoes

This pot pie marries the salty tanginess of soy sauce with the mellow bite of baked potatoes. It's the perfect meal to serve when you want something wholesome but not too heavy. The tofu boosts the protein content, and the bounty of vegetables is guaranteed to help you hit your daily allotment of whole-food goodness. The addition of nutritional yeast (found at health-food stores and specialty grocery stores) is key here. It adds a rich, cheesy flavor to the whole pie that really takes the taste up a notch.

Note: *Unless stated, you do not need to chop or slice the vegetables into one precise size, but make sure the pieces are all bite-sized.*

Makes 2 very large or 4 individual servings

7 oz. extra-firm tofu (½ package)
3 Tbsp. olive oil, divided
1 small yellow onion, diced
2 large celery stalks, sliced
1 large carrot, sliced
2 garlic cloves, crushed
1 medium-sized baking potato, cubed but not peeled
½ cup green beans, cut
½ cup mushrooms, sliced
¼ cup whole-wheat flour
2 tsp. nutritional yeast
1½ Tbsp. soy sauce
1¼ cups vegetable broth
1 tsp. dried sage
1 tsp. dried marjoram
¼ tsp. dried basil
salt and pepper to taste

Crust
½ cup all-purpose white flour
½ cup whole-wheat flour
1 tsp. salt
⅓ cup vegan "butter," very cold
4 to 6 Tbsp. ice water

1 Preheat the oven to 400 degrees F. Drain the tofu, and cut into cubes. Heat 1 Tbsp. olive oil in a large skillet over medium heat, and cook the tofu until golden on all sides — about 5 minutes. Remove the tofu from the skillet, and set aside.

2 Heat the remaining olive oil in the same skillet. Add the onion, celery, carrot and garlic, and sauté until the onion becomes translucent — about 5 minutes. Add the potato and the rest of the vegetables, stirring frequently until tender but not mushy — about 7 minutes.

3 Add the flour, nutritional yeast and soy sauce to the skillet. Stir. Add the vegetable broth, and stir until combined, scraping the browned bits from the bottom of the pan.

4 Add the cooked tofu and spices, stirring until combined. Remove from the heat, and season to taste with salt and pepper.

5 Pour the mixture into a baking dish, and let the filling sit while you make the crust. I've used an oval baking dish (9-by-12 inches, roughly); any similar vessel will work well. If you choose to make the pot pie in individual ramekins, portion the dough by rolling it out and cutting out shapes to cover the tops of the pies.

6 In a large bowl, mix the two flours along with the salt. Add the buttery spread, and cut it into the flour using a butter knife or pastry cutter. Mix in the water 1 Tbsp. at a time until the mixture forms a ball. Knead with your hands, and place on a floured surface. Roll thin (about ¼- to ⅛-inch thick), and place over the vegetable-filled baking dish. Pinch the sides to form an edge.

7 Bake for 30 minutes until golden and bubbly. Cool for 5 minutes; then serve.

Gluten-free Goodies

RECIPES AND PHOTOS BY WENDY BEDWELL-WILSON

for those who avoid gluten, these hearty recipes can make ideal replacements.

Gluten-free Chicken Pot Pie with Rosemary and Citrus

What is it about chicken seasoned with rosemary and citrus? The woody, fragrant rosemary marries perfectly with the sweet, tart citrus, flavoring the chicken and making it juicy and delicious. When those tantalizing tastes are combined with vegetables and enrobed in a buttery gluten-free crust, the result is the ultimate wheat-free comfort food.

Here, you'll find three recipes: a gluten-free flour blend for use in the crust, the gluten-free pastry crust, and the pot pie itself.

Makes 4 to 6 servings

Gluten-free flour blend
3 cups brown rice flour
1⅛ cups potato starch (*not* potato flour)
⅜ cup tapioca starch
2½ tsp. xanthan gum

Add all of the ingredients to a bowl, and mix well. Use immediately or store in an airtight container in the freezer for up to 6 months.

Crust *(makes both top and bottom crusts)*
2½ cups gluten-free flour blend (use the recipe listed above)
1 tsp. sea salt
2 sticks (16 Tbsp.) unsalted butter, cut into ½-inch cubes and frozen overnight

7 to 9 Tbsp. ice water
1 egg white
2 Tbsp. butter, melted

1 Add the flour and salt to the food processor. Pulse to mix well. Add the frozen butter, and pulse several times, scraping the sides and bottom with a spatula, as needed, until the mixture forms the size of peas and smaller. Add 1 Tbsp. ice water at a time, pulsing between additions. Use the least amount of water possible; too much water will create a tough crust. Stop pulsing before it forms dough but once it sticks together when pinched.

2 Transfer the dough to a flat surface lined with parchment paper and very lightly dusted with flour. With the palm of your hand, flatten and mold the dough to form a ½-inch-thick disk. It will appear crumbly at first; continued manipulation will soften the butter and hold the mixture together.

3 Cut the disk in half. Reshape each half into its own disk. Dust lightly with the flour mixture. Wrap each one separately in plastic wrap, and refrigerate for 1 to 48 hours.

4 Remove 1 disk from the refrigerator, and let it rest at room temperature for 5 minutes. Using gentle pressure and a flour-dusted rolling pin, roll out

Pot Pie

⅓ cup butter
1 cup carrots, coarsely chopped
1 cup diced potatoes
½ cup frozen peas
1 cup chopped onion
1 large garlic clove
1½ tsp. fresh rosemary
1 cup celery
½ cup diced celery
2 cups cooked chicken, cut into bite-sized pieces
3 Tbsp. brown rice flour
1⅓ cups gluten-free chicken broth
⅔ cup milk or unsweetened, unflavored almond milk
3 Tbsp. fresh squeezed orange juice
salt and pepper to taste
1 recipe gluten-free pie crust (far left)

the disk onto a parchment-paper-lined, lightly flour-dusted surface to approximately ⅛ inch thick and 12 inches round. If holes form, reseal them by gently pinching the dough and rolling it.

5 To flip the crust into your 9-inch pie pan, place the pan upside down on the crust, and hold it with one hand. Slide your other hand under the parchment paper, carefully lift the crust and pan, and gently flip them over. Press the crust into the bottom and sides of the pie pan with a ¼-inch to ½-inch edge overlapping the rim. Baste the crust with egg white to prevent a soggy bottom. Fill the crust with filling (see recipe to the right).

6 Roll out the second disk for the top of your pot pie by using the same method as above. When it's approximately ⅛ inch thick, slide your hand under the parchment paper, and flip the crust onto the top of the filled pie, making sure it completely covers the filling. Seal it to the lower crust by using a fork to crimp the edges.

7 Cut several slits in the top of the pie crust to allow steam to escape and prevent a soggy crust. Baste the top of the crust with the egg white, and bake as directed. Baste the pot pie with melted butter every 10 minutes or so until it becomes golden-brown.

1 Preheat the oven to 350 degrees F. Add the butter to a deep skillet, and melt on medium heat. Add the carrots, and sauté over low heat for 10 minutes. Add the potatoes, peas, onion, garlic, rosemary and celery. Stir and sauté for 8 minutes or until soft.

2 Add chicken to the vegetable mixture. Stir, and heat through. Add flour, and stir until the vegetables and chicken are coated. Slowly add the chicken broth, almond milk and orange juice, and bring to a boil. Stir until thickened. Add salt and pepper to taste. Fill your prepared pie crust with filling.

3 Prepare and place the second pie crust on top of the pot pie. As mentioned to the left, seal by crimping with a fork, cut slits in the top, and coat the top with egg white. Bake for 50 minutes, basting every 10 minutes with butter. When the top is golden-brown and the filling is hot, remove from the oven. Cool for at least 10 minutes before serving.

Gluten-free Shepherd's Pie
with Lamb and Bacon ///

Made with a buttery potato crust rather than a pastry crust, a shepherd's pie is by nature gluten-free (as long as you use rice flour instead of all-purpose flour for the gravy). To take a traditional pub-food favorite to the next level, we've added a dash of bacon goodness to the rich lamb and vegetable blend.

Yields 4 to 6 servings

1½ lbs. russet potatoes, peeled and quartered (about 2 medium- to large-sized)
1 Tbsp. butter
½ cup chicken broth
salt and pepper to taste
3 Tbsp. olive oil
1 medium onion, chopped
1 cup carrots, chopped

1 cup celery, chopped
2 garlic cloves, chopped
½ cup frozen corn
½ cup frozen peas
2 cups finely chopped cooked lamb or 1 lb. raw ground lamb
2 Tbsp. brown rice flour
1 ½ cup beef or chicken broth
1 Tbsp. Worcestershire sauce
1 Tbsp. tomato paste
½ cup cooked bacon, crumbled
½ tsp. dried thyme or 1½ tsp. chopped fresh thyme
½ tsp. dried rosemary or 1½ tsp. chopped fresh rosemary
pinch of grated or ground nutmeg
salt and black pepper to taste
2 Tbsp. butter, cut into small pieces

1 Place the potatoes in large pot of cold water. Bring to a boil over medium heat, and cook until tender — about 15 minutes. Drain. Put through a ricer or mash with a fork.

2 Add the butter, chicken broth, salt and pepper, and mix well until combined and fluffy. Set aside. Preheat the oven to 400 degrees F.

3 Heat olive oil in a large skillet. Add onion, carrots, celery and garlic. Cook over medium heat until tender. Add corn and peas, and heat through.

4 Increase the heat, and add the lamb. If using cooked lamb, stir until the meat begins to brown — about 5 minutes. If using raw lamb, cook it (breaking up the meat with a spoon) until the lamb loses its pink color — about 5 to 10 minutes. Spoon off excess fat.

5 Stir in the rice flour to coat the meat and vegetables. Add the broth, Worcestershire, tomato paste, bacon, thyme, rosemary, nutmeg, salt and pepper. Reduce the heat and cook, stirring occasionally, until thickened — about 5 minutes.

6 Transfer to an 8-by-8-inch greased baking dish or 9-inch pie pan. Spread the mashed potatoes over the top, making peaks with a fork. Scatter the butter chunks evenly over the top. Place the pan on top of a cooking sheet. Bake until the potatoes appear browned and the dish is heated through — about 30 to 35 minutes. Let cool slightly; then serve directly from the baking dish.

Breakfast Pies

RECIPES AND PHOTOS BY ASHLEY ENGLISH

start
your day off right. Eat pie for breakfast!

Breakfast-sausage-hash Pot Pie

Potato and sausage hash makes a common breakfast entrée. In this recipe, I've cradled rich, buttery pastry around the hash filling. The result is a breakfast pot pie that'll have you saluting the dawn!

Makes 1 8-by-8-inch pot pie

Basic pot-pie crust
2½ cups all-purpose flour
1¼ tsp. salt
1 cup butter (2 sticks), chilled and cubed
¾ cup ice water

Hash filling
1½ lbs. sweet potatoes (or medium starch white potatoes), peeled and cubed
1 medium red onion, diced
1 red pepper, diced
1 carrot, peeled and diced
1 fennel bulb, including the fronds, sliced into small pieces
2 Tbsp. vegetable oil or lard
3 garlic cloves, minced
1½ lbs. uncooked, ground breakfast sausage
½ tsp. sea salt
black pepper to taste
1 egg yolk, beaten

1 Mix the flour and salt in a medium-sized bowl. Using a pastry cutter or two forks, incorporate the butter until the mixture resembles a coarse meal but with several pea- and lima-bean-sized bits in the mix.

2 Slowly drizzle in the ice water. Stir with a mixing spoon until the dough starts to clump. Transfer the dough onto a floured work surface, and fold it into itself using your hands. The dough should come together easily but shouldn't feel overly sticky.

3 Divide the dough in half, and shape into two flattened disks. Wrap each disk in plastic, and refrigerate for at least 1 hour.

4 Preheat the oven to 400 degrees Fahrenheit. Remove one of the dough disks from the refrigerator. Using a rolling pin, shape it into a square on a lightly floured surface.

5 Transfer the dough to an 8-by-8-inch baking pan. Trim the overhang to 1 inch. Prick the bottom of the crust 6 to 7 times with the tines of a fork. Place the crust in the refrigerator to chill for 15 minutes.

6 Line the crust with parchment paper, and fill with dried beans or pie weights. Bake for 10 minutes. Set aside. Remove the pie weights and parchment once cool enough to handle. Reduce oven temperature to 375 degrees F.

7 Next, prepare the filling. Brown the sausage in a heavy-bottomed pan over medium heat until cooked through — about 8 to 10 minutes. Remove the sausage from the pan, and set aside.

8 Place the oil or lard into the hot pan. Add the sweet potatoes, onion, red pepper, carrot and fennel. Cook for 20 to 25 minutes or until the vegetables become lightly browned and cooked through. Add the garlic, and cook for 2 to 3 minutes. Add the sausage, and cook for 2 minutes. Season with salt and pepper.

9 Transfer the mixture into the crust-lined pan. Roll the remaining dough disk into a square. Using a knife, cut 4 to 6 2-inch slits across the top of the dough, creating steam vents.

10 Transfer the top crust over the filling. Trim the top crust to a 1-inch overhang. Tuck the edges of the top crust under the bottom crust, and crimp the edges decoratively. Using a pastry brush, brush the top of the crust with the egg.

11 Bake for 30 to 35 minutes until the crust appears golden-brown. Cool 15 minutes before serving.

Smoked Salmon, Spinach and Potato Pie

This pot pie takes three savory flavors often enjoyed at breakfast and marries them in one exquisite trinity. An egg base is layered with crispy potato slices, smothered with a thick spinach-and-cream-cheese topping and covered in smoked salmon.

Makes 1 9-inch deep-dish pot pie

Pie crust
½ recipe basic pot pie crust
  (page 63)

Egg layer
12 large eggs
¼ cup half-and-half
pinch of sea salt
dash of hot sauce
1 tsp. dill

Potato layer
1 lb. potatoes, cut into ⅓-inch-thick disks
2 Tbsp. vegetable oil (preferably coconut)

Spinach and cream cheese layer
10 oz. frozen spinach
8 oz. cream cheese at room temperature
pinch of sea salt
black pepper to taste
½ tsp. granulated garlic
½ tsp. dill

Topping
4 oz. smoked salmon, cut into bite-size pieces
1 Tbsp. capers
1 oz. crumbled feta, if desired

1 Begin by preparing the pie crust. Follow instructions in the recipe on page 63, reducing the ingredient

quantities by half. You also can make the full recipe and keep the other half for later use.

2 Use a 9-inch deep-dish pie pan, and roll the dough into a circle. Place the crust into the pie pan, and trim to a 1-inch overhang. Tuck under the edges of the crust, and crimp the edges decoratively. Prick the bottom of the crust 6 or 7 times; proceed according to the rest of the directions on page 63. Set the prepared crust aside, and reduce the oven temperature to 360 degrees F.

3 Next, prepare the egg layer. Whisk the eggs, half-and-half, salt, hot sauce and dill in a medium-sized bowl until fully incorporated. Pour the mixture into the prepared crust. Bake for 30 minutes.

4 In a large pan, cook potatoes over medium-high heat in the oil for about 12 minutes, turning occasionally, until browned and cooked through. Remove from the pan. Cut the disks in half.

5 Cook the spinach according to the package instructions. Transfer to a medium-sized mixing bowl, and stir in the cream cheese, salt, pepper, garlic and dill until fully incorporated. Set aside.

6 After the egg layer has baked, remove the pie from the oven, and top it with the cooked potato slices. Return to the oven, and bake for 5 minutes.

7 Remove the pie from the oven. Gently spoon the cream-cheese mixture on top, and smooth it over with a spoon or spatula.

8 Arrange the salmon pieces on top of the pie. Sprinkle the capers evenly over the salmon. Top with crumbled feta, if desired.

Apple and Biscuit Pot Pie

As a child, my mom's go-to weekend breakfast often contained sautéed apples and biscuits. Here, I've combined the two into one sweet, hearty breakfast pot pie.

Makes 1 8-by-8-inch pot pie

Apple filling
3 lbs. apples, peeled, cored, quartered and sliced into ½-inch pieces (I suggest Gala, Fuji, Pink Lady, Stayman or Honeycrisp.)
⅓ cup dark brown sugar
¼ cup raisins
2 Tbsp. all-purpose flour
1 tsp. ground cinnamon
½ tsp. ground ginger
½ tsp. ground nutmeg
¼ tsp. ground allspice
juice of 1 lemon
pinch of sea salt

Biscuit topping
1 cup all-purpose flour
1 tsp. baking powder
¼ tsp. baking soda
¼ tsp. sea salt
3 Tbsp. butter, cubed
¾ cup buttermilk
3 Tbsp. butter, melted

1 Preheat the oven to 400 degrees F. Place the apple slices, brown sugar, raisins, flour, spices, lemon juice and salt in a medium-sized mixing bowl. Using a mixing spoon or clean hands, toss until all of the ingredients are fully combined and the apples are evenly coated in flour, sugar and spices. Set aside.

2 In a medium-sized mixing bowl, combine the flour, baking powder, baking soda and salt. Using a pastry cutter or fork, cut in the butter cubes until the mixture becomes crumbly and the butter appears pea-sized or smaller.

3 Create a well in the center of the mixture. Pour in the buttermilk. Using a mixing spoon, gently incorporate the milk just until all of the dry ingredients appear moistened. The mixture will look quite wet at this point, but that's fine.

4 Place the apple mixture into an 8-by-8-inch baking pan. Using a spoon, add dollops of the biscuit topping on top of the apples, aiming for mounds of about 3 Tbsp. in quantity. Pour the melted butter over the biscuit topping.

5 Bake for 15 minutes. Reduce the oven temperature to 350 degrees F, and continue baking for 20 to 25 minutes or until the biscuit topping turns golden-brown. Cool for at least 15 minutes before serving.

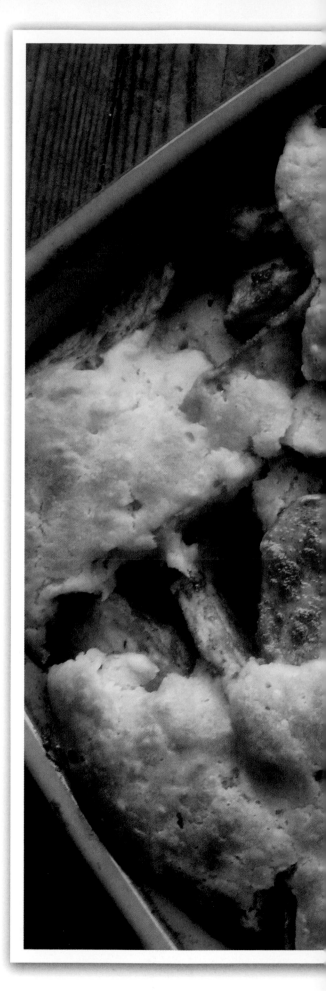

International Pies

RECIPES AND PHOTOS BY FIONA GREEN

bring foreign flavor to your kitchen.

MASHE/SHUTTERSTOCK

Thai Curried Chicken Pot Pie

My Vietnamese friend, Thuy, explained that in her country, curry is often topped with bread dough which cooks up in the oven, providing warm, fresh bread with which to mop up the sauce at the end of the meal. Here we offer a twist by using Thai red curry and replacing the bread with a puff-pastry topping. The result is delicious with the crispy pastry perfectly complementing the spicy curry. Feel free to experiment with your favorite spices.

Serves 2 to 4

1½ lbs. chicken, cubed
1 Tbsp. lemon juice
4 tsp. red curry paste

2 Tbsp. basil oil
3 shallots, sliced
2 garlic cloves, crushed
3 medium carrots, sliced
4 celery stalks, sliced
1 large potato, diced
1 cup coconut milk
1½ cups chicken broth
8 oz. puff pastry
1 egg white, beaten

1 Place the cubed chicken in a bowl with the lemon juice and curry paste, mix well, and marinate in the refrigerator for 30 minutes.

2 In a frying pan, heat the basil oil, and cook the shallots and garlic for 2 minutes until slightly soft. Add the chicken. Continue to cook on medium heat, stirring occasionally, until the chicken is cooked through — about 5 minutes.

3 Add the carrots, celery, potato, coconut milk and chicken broth, and stir. Reduce the heat to low, and simmer for 20 minutes until the vegetables have absorbed the curry. Set aside to cool.

4 Preheat the oven to 375 degrees Fahrenheit. When the curry filling has cooled, ladle it into a 9-by-5-inch casserole dish.

5 Trim the pastry to fit over the top of the casserole dish, overlapping the edges slightly. Brush the top lightly with the egg white, and cut a few slits in the pastry to allow steam to escape.

6 Place the dish on the middle shelf of the oven, and cook for 30 to 35 minutes or until the pastry looks nicely browned.

7 Remove from the oven, and cool for about 5 minutes. Serve with rice if desired.

Layered Chicken Tamale Pie

In this recipe, a layer of delicious cornbread tops spicy chicken, beans and cheese to create a hearty family meal. It includes mild bell peppers; for an extra kick, you might consider using one poblano pepper and one bell pepper. For a vegetarian alternative, replace the meat in this recipe with extra beans, peppers and sun-dried tomatoes.

Serves 4 to 6

1 15-oz. can pinto or black beans
¼ cup chopped fresh cilantro

2 Tbsp. chipotle pepper powder, divided
pinch of salt
pinch of ground black pepper
1 lb. chicken filets, cut into strips
2 Tbsp. basil oil
1 medium onion, sliced
2 bell peppers, sliced
¼ cup sliced, pickled jalapeños
2 cups grated mozzarella cheese, divided

Cornmeal base and topping
1½ cups coarse-grind cornmeal
2 cups chicken broth
2 cups water
1 tsp. salt
1 tsp. paprika
4 Tbsp. butter
1 Tbsp. chipotle pepper powder

Garnish
chopped fresh cilantro
grated mozzarella cheese

1 Grease an 8-by-8-inch casserole dish with butter, and set aside. In a small bowl, mix the beans, cilantro, 1 Tbsp. chipotle pepper powder, salt and pepper. Set aside.

2 Cook the chicken in basil oil for about 7 minutes until cooked through. Add the onion, peppers, jalapeño and 1 Tbsp. chipotle pepper powder, and cook for 10 minutes or until vegetables become slightly soft. Remove from the heat.

3 Preheat the oven to 375 degrees F. To prepare the cornbread, mix the cornmeal, broth, water, salt and paprika in a large pot. Bring to a boil, reduce the heat, and simmer for 10 minutes. Add the butter, and stir until melted.

4 Pour half of the cornmeal mix into the casserole dish, distributing evenly. Sprinkle 1 cup cheese over the cornmeal mix. Top with a layer of the bean mixture. Add the remaining cheese. Evenly distribute the chicken over the cheese layer. Finish with the remaining cornmeal mix. Sprinkle chipotle pepper powder on top, and place the uncovered dish in the oven.

5 Cook for 35 minutes. Remove from the oven, and cool for 5 minutes. Garnish with cilantro and grated cheese. Serve with sour cream, salsa and baked tortilla chips.

Greek Spanakopita with Sun-dried Tomatoes

One of my favorite Greek dishes is spanakopita, a delicious spinach-and-cheese pie prepared with herbs and spices. In this twist on the classic recipe, sun-dried tomatoes add an extra burst of flavor. While dill is often the herb of choice in Greece, this recipe uses herbes de Provence. Feel free to experiment with your favorite herbs to create your own signature dish.

Makes 4 individual pies

6 oz. fresh spinach, chopped
½ cup sun-dried tomatoes, chopped
1 Tbsp. olive oil
½ medium onion, chopped
¼ cup fresh parsley, chopped
1 Tbsp. herbes de Provence
pinch of salt
pinch of ground black pepper
1 egg
½ cup ricotta cheese
1 cup crumbled feta cheese
9 sheets phyllo dough (13-by-17 inches)
½ cup olive oil for basting the sheets of phyllo dough
1 beaten egg for the glaze
2 Tbsp. sesame seeds

1 Combine the spinach and sun-dried tomatoes in a bowl. Set aside.

2 Heat the oil in a large pan, and lightly fry the onion for 4 minutes. Add the spinach mixture to the pan, and cook for about 3 minutes until the spinach starts to wilt. Remove from the heat, drain the excess liquid through a colander, and set aside to cool. Once cool, add the parsley, herbes de Provence, salt and pepper.

3 In a bowl, beat the egg; then stir in the ricotta and feta cheeses. Add to the cooled spinach mixture. Mix well, and set aside. Preheat the oven to 375 degrees F.

4 Take 1 sheet of phyllo dough, and baste with olive oil. Place a second sheet on top of the first sheet, and baste it with olive oil. Repeat with the remaining layers.

5 Cut the pastry stack in half vertically and horizontally to form 4 squares. Place ¼ of the filling on the top half of 1 square. Brush the edges of the square with beaten egg; then fold the corner over to form a sealed triangle.

6 Trim off any excess pastry; then place the triangle on the greased baking sheet. Repeat these two steps with the other squares. Baste the tops of the triangles with beaten egg. Sprinkle with sesame seeds if desired.

7 Bake for 20 to 25 minutes or until the pastry turns a delicate golden-brown color. Remove from the oven, cool for a few minutes, and enjoy.

Scottish Smoked Salmon Pasty

This recipe has been passed down from generation to generation in our family. Smoked haddock is often chosen as the fish of choice, but I love to use honey-smoked salmon, too. Its sweet flavor pairs well with the light, fluffy potatoes and crispy puff pastry. Regular smoked salmon or any smoked fish can be used. Serve with a light salad of arugula, tomato and cucumber with a honey-mustard dressing.

Serves 2 to 4

1 Tbsp. butter
6 Tbsp. milk
8 oz. honey-smoked salmon, crumbled
2 cups boiled, mashed potatoes
2 green onions, sliced
1 hard-boiled egg, chopped
½ cup chopped cilantro
½ tsp. nutmeg
salt and pepper to taste

8 oz. puff pastry
4 Tbsp. milk to glaze the pastry

1 Preheat the oven to 375 degrees F. Melt the butter in a saucepan; then pour it into a bowl with the milk.

2 Add the salmon, potatoes, green onions, egg, cilantro, nutmeg, salt and pepper. Mix well, and set aside to cool.

3 Roll out the pastry to form a 10-inch square. Place the filling in the center of the square. Brush the edges of the pastry with some of the milk, and fold the corners into the center so they overlap slightly and form an envelope. Glaze the top of the pastry with the remaining milk.

4 Place the parcel in the oven, and bake for 40 to 45 minutes or until golden-brown. Remove from the oven. Cool for 5 minutes, and cut into portions.

Shepherd's Pie

Many countries have their own version of shepherd's pie, a delicious dish originally created to use leftover meat. In the United Kingdom, lamb is often used, while in France and Portugal, beef generally remains the meat of choice. This recipe, which combines turkey with buttery white potatoes and maple-flavored sweet potatoes, is guaranteed to have everyone asking for more.

Serves 2 to 4

2 large carrots, sliced
2 parsnips, sliced
2 large sweet potatoes
2 large white potatoes
2 Tbsp. butter
1 Tbsp. sour cream
1 tsp. salt
2 Tbsp. maple syrup
1 cup frozen sweet peas
1 lb. cooked turkey, cut into bite-sized chunks
1 cup turkey gravy

1 Bring a large pot of water to boiling, and add the carrots and parsnips. Boil for approximately 10 minutes until tender.

2 Meanwhile, in separate pots of boiling water, boil the sweet potatoes and white potatoes for 10 minutes or until soft. Remove from the heat.

3 Smash the white potatoes in a bowl, and mix in the butter, sour cream and salt. Smash the sweet potatoes in a separate bowl, and mix in the maple syrup.

4 Preheat the oven to 350 degrees F. Place the carrots, parsnips and peas in a rectangular 9-by-5-inch casserole dish.

5 Top with the turkey chunks. Pour the turkey gravy over the meat. Top with the potatoes, alternating colors to form stripes.

6 Bake for 30 minutes. Remove from the oven, and cool for 5 minutes before serving.

French Canadian Tourtière //////////////////////////////

Tourtière, a savory meat pie, is traditionally enjoyed by French Canadians during the winter months, particularly on Christmas Eve and New Year's Eve. Countless variations exist; some use beef, pork, veal or turkey, and others use a combination of meats. We use pork in this recipe, and instead of making one single shortcrust pie, we make three pies using both shortcrust and puff pastry.

In Québec, the pie is generally served with some form of homemade sweet ketchup; however, any tomato-based relish or chili sauce makes an excellent substitute.

Makes 3 individual pies

1 large potato, diced
1 tsp. olive oil
1 lb. ground pork
1 medium onion, chopped
1 large carrot, diced
1 garlic clove, minced
2 celery stalks, sliced
1 cup chicken broth
3 bacon slices (optional), chopped
1 tsp. cinnamon
1 tsp. ground allspice
2 Tbsp. fresh parsley
8 oz. regular, all-purpose pastry dough (recipe appears on page 14)
8 oz. puff pastry
1 tsp. dried rosemary
1 beaten egg for egg wash

1 Grease 3 6-inch, individual, round casserole dishes.

2 Bring a pot of water to boil, and add the potato. Boil until soft — approximately 7 minutes. Remove from the heat, and set aside.

3 In a saucepan, heat the oil over medium heat. Add the pork, and cook for approximately 8 minutes until cooked through.

4 Drain the fat; then add the onion, carrot, garlic, celery, broth, bacon, cinnamon and allspice, and bring to a boil. Reduce the heat, and simmer for 30 minutes. Remove from the heat. Add the parsley and potato. Mix well, set aside, and cool.

5 Preheat the oven to 400 degrees F. Roll out the pastry, and shape into 3 circles. These will cover the base and sides of your casserole dishes. Place the pastry inside the dishes, and trim any excess.

6 Place parchment paper inside the dishes, and weigh it down with dehydrated beans. Precook the pastry for 10 minutes.

7 While the pastry bakes, cut the puff pastry into 3 7-inch rounds, which will slightly overlap the rims of the casserole dishes. Keep refrigerated until ready to use.

8 Remove the casserole dishes from the oven, and reduce the oven temperature to 350 degrees F. Remove the parchment paper and beans.

9 Fill the pie shells with the cooled meat filling, and top with the puff pastry lids. Baste the pastry with the egg wash, cut a slit in the top to allow steam to escape, and return the casserole dishes to the oven.

10 Bake for 25 minutes or until the pastry turns a nice, golden-brown color. Serve with the fruity ketchup or chutney of your choice.

Sweet Treats

RECIPES AND PHOTOS BY FIONA GREEN

dessert
pies make the perfect dough-covered delight.

Cranberry and White Chocolate Empanadas

Bite-sized pockets of buttery, melt-in-your-mouth pastry envelop tart cranberries and creamy white chocolate. Served warm with ice cream or whipped cream, these tasty treats are sure to be a crowd-pleaser.

Makes 18 miniature empanadas

Cranberry filling
2 cups fresh cranberries
½ cup orange or apple juice
½ cup brown sugar
1 cup white chocolate chips

Pastry
1¼ cups flour
¼ cup finely granulated sugar
8 oz. butter
2 egg yolks (save the egg whites for the egg wash)
2 Tbsp. water

2 Tbsp. powdered or brown sugar

1. In a small saucepan, combine the cranberries, fruit juice and sugar. Bring to a boil, reduce the heat, and simmer for approximately 15 minutes or until the cranberries have popped and become mushy.

2. Remove from the heat. Mash the cranberries with a fork, stir in the chocolate chips, and mix well. Set aside to cool.

3. In a food processor, mix the flour, sugar, butter, egg yolks and water until a soft, pliable dough forms. If the dough does not become pliable, add water in increments of 1 tsp. Wrap the pastry dough in plastic, and refrigerate for at least 40 minutes.

4. Preheat the oven to 350 degrees Fahrenheit. Remove the pastry dough from the refrigerator, and roll out until just thick enough to hold together. With a cookie cutter, cut 18 circles of approximately 3 inches in diameter.

5. Place the cranberry filling on half of each circle; then baste the edges of the circle with water. Fold over the pastry to form a semi-circle, and seal well using the blunt edge of a knife. Baste with beaten egg whites.

6. Bake for approximately 15 minutes. Remove from the oven, and dust with powdered or brown sugar. Cool for 10 minutes before serving with whipped cream.

Apricot and Almond Baklava

Dried apricots, cardamom and orange blossom water create a unique taste sensation sure to impress friends and family. This recipe uses almonds and pistachios; however, any nuts can be used.

Serves 8

Syrup
½ cup agave nectar
½ cup honey
2 Tbsp. apricot nectar
2 tsp. cardamom
1 tsp. orange peel
3 Tbsp. orange blossom water

Filling
5 dried apricots, finely chopped
1 cup chopped almonds
1 Tbsp. cardamom
1 Tbsp. brown sugar

24 phyllo pastry sheets (13-by-17 inches)
8 Tbsp. (1 stick) butter
2 Tbsp. honey, divided
2 Tbsp. ground pistachios for decoration

1 In a saucepan, combine the agave nectar, honey, apricot nectar, cardamom, orange peel and orange blossom water. Bring to a boil; then reduce the temperature, and simmer for 5 minutes. Remove from the heat, and set aside to cool.

2 Preheat the oven to 350 degrees F. Prepare the nut filling by mixing the apricots and almonds with the cardamom and brown sugar. Set aside.

3 Grease a 9-by-13-inch casserole dish. Trim the phyllo sheets to fit the dish.

4 Melt the butter in a small saucepan. Place 1 sheet of phyllo pastry in the casserole dish. Evenly brush the sheet with melted butter. Place a second sheet on top, and baste this sheet with melted butter. Repeat 6 times.

5 Spread half of the filling over the pastry stack. Drizzle 1 Tbsp. honey over the filling. Cover with a sheet of pastry. Baste with melted butter, and repeat with 7 sheets. Spread the remaining mixture evenly over the pastry stack, drizzle the remaining honey over the nuts, and finish with 8 pastry sheets, buttering after each sheet is added.

6 Spritz the top layer with a light mist of water to prevent the pastry from curling in the oven. Cut into diamonds with a knife, and place on the lower shelf of the oven. Bake for 40 minutes.

7 Remove from the oven, and carefully spoon the syrup over the baklava. Sprinkle the ground pistachios on top, and cool for at least 2 hours. Serve with tea or coffee as a mid-afternoon treat.

Mini Pluot and Raspberry Crumble Pies

These individual crumble pies taste delicious hot from the oven as well as cold the next day. The recipe uses pluots, a cross between a plum and an apricot.

Thanks to the natural sweetness of this fruit, the dish does not require much extra sugar. If pluots are not available, plums can be used.

Makes 3 5-inch pies

Fruit filling
6 ripe pluots
12 oz. ripe raspberries
1 Tbsp. cinnamon
1 Tbsp. flour
1 Tbsp. brown sugar
2 Tbsp. lemon juice

Crumble topping
⅔ cup all-purpose flour
½ cup brown sugar
4 Tbsp. butter, chilled and diced
¾ cup sliced almonds

all-purpose dough (page 14)

1 Preheat the oven to 400 degrees F. To prepare the fruit filling, peel the pluots, and cut into walnut-sized pieces. Place in a bowl with the raspberries. Add the cinnamon, flour, sugar and lemon juice, mix, and set aside.

2 Prepare the crumble topping by mixing the flour, sugar and butter. Add the almonds, and mix well.

3 Grease 3 5-inch casserole dishes with butter. Cut the pastry into circles large enough to cover the bottom and sides of pots. Smooth out evenly in the dishes.

4 Place parchment paper inside the dishes, and weigh down with dehydrated beans. Precook the pastry bases for 10 minutes. Remove the pastries from the oven, and remove the paper and beans. Spoon the prepared fruit into the pastry cups, and cover with the crumble topping.

5 Return to the oven, and bake for 10 minutes or until the crumble topping looks nicely browned. Cool for 5 minutes before serving with vanilla ice cream or whipped cream.

Amaretto-flavored Peach and Mango Cobbler

When it comes to comfort food, nothing beats a warm fruit cobbler. Here, peaches and mangos are soaked in amaretto and mixed for a totally tropical taste, while coconut milk in the cobbler topping replaces regular milk. This dessert tastes delicious with coconut ice cream or whipped cream. Peaches and mangos can vary in size; plan on using 4 cups of fruit.

Serves 6

Fruit filling
2 large, ripe peaches
2 large, ripe mangos
¼ cup amaretto
2 Tbsp. lemon juice
2 Tbsp. brown sugar
1 Tbsp. flour

Topping
1 cup brown sugar
1 cup flour
1 tsp. baking powder
1 tsp. cinnamon
1 cup coconut milk
4 Tbsp. butter
1 Tbsp. brown sugar

1 Preheat the oven to 375 degrees F. Peel and chop the fruit, and place it in a bowl with the amaretto, lemon juice, sugar and flour. Mix well, and set aside for 30 minutes.

2 In a separate bowl, mix the sugar, flour, baking powder, cinnamon and coconut milk for the topping. Set aside.

3 Melt the butter in a small saucepan. Pour the melted butter into a 9-by-12-inch casserole dish. Spoon the fruit into the dish, and top with the cobbler batter. Sprinkle brown sugar over the top of the batter.

4 Bake the cobbler on the lower shelf of the oven for 40 minutes or until the top appears nicely browned and the fruit starts to bubble through. Remove from the oven, and cool for 5 minutes before serving with whipped cream or ice cream.

WHAT MAKES A Pot Pie Great?

pie maven and "A Year of Pies: A Seasonal Tour of Home Baked Pies" (Lark Crafts) author Ashley English says the true ingredients to a fabulous pot pie boil down to a few requisites: fat, metal and freshness.

For starters, an amazing pot pie begins with an amazing crust. "Though the filling is the actor in the spotlight," English says, "the crust plays an indispensable supporting role, leaving the most lasting impression well after the meal has passed." To achieve that "buttery, flaky, delectable pot pie," an all-butter or lard crust is a must. Start with good fats, and you're halfway to a perfect pot pie.

In the English kitchen, wooden rolling pins and food processors are set aside in favor of metal and elbow grease. "A sturdy rolling pin and a pastry cutter are my go-to tools," she says. A metal rolling pin keeps dough from sticking. English's pastry dough is made by hand with the assistance of a pastry cutter, which quickly cuts the butter into the flour.

Crust is all well and good, but what about the main event? The star of the culinary show? When it comes to the filling, English looks to the calendar. "The seasons are my perennial culinary guide," she says. "Fruits and vegetables simply taste better in the season they grow in wherever one lives."

Using the freshest in-season produce as a springboard, English weaves the tradition of tried-and-true flavor pairings with her own inspiration. "From there, I look for flavor pairings that historically go well together and then seek out a creative twist to give it a bit of flair and edge." English's recipes appear on page 62.

Kristina Mercedes Urquhart writes from the mountains of western North Carolina. Follow her exploits at kristinamercedes.tumblr.com

KEVIN FOGLE

You can perfect your pie with these pointers.

BY KRISTINA MERCEDES URQUHART

FOR A RAINY DAY

Successfully store, freeze and reheat your homemade pot pies.

BY KEVIN FOGLE

the ease and convenience of store-bought frozen pot pies remain unmatched. Unfortunately, the taste and quality of these mass-produced offerings pale in comparison to the homemade variety. The good news is that when creating this classic comfort food at home, you can make enough for several meals or even freeze pot pies for the future while saving time and money in the process.

Doubling a recipe and freezing the leftovers allows for a quick, easy meal later on.

MSPHOTOGRAPHIC/SHUTTERSTOCK

KEVIN FOGLE

The Leftover Quandary

Easy and delicious, leftover pot pie can make an additional meal or two for your household. While leftovers have a negative association in many homes, day-old pot pie has the ability to change minds when stored and reheated properly.

STORING YOUR LEFTOVERS

Refrigerate any leftovers within an hour of eating to reduce the risk of bacterial contamination. When dealing with larger pot pies, divide the dish into smaller portions to speed up the cooling process.

Place leftovers in air-tight containers or foil packets to retain moisture. Keeping air away from the pot pie also will prevent oxidation and unwanted food odors from taking over the refrigerator, which can cause the off-flavors commonly associated with leftovers.

With food safety in mind, refrigerated leftovers should be consumed within three to four days at most.

THE REHEATING PROCESS

Ovens provide the best results when reheating leftover pot pie. Use foil packets with the crust exposed, or place a serving in a small ramekin dish to keep the pot-pie filling moist while allowing the crust to crisp. Slow heating — between 325 to 375 degrees Fahrenheit until heated through — is best for the integrity of the leftovers.

The United States Department of Agriculture recommends that all leftovers be reheated to an internal temperature of 165 degrees F. Consider using an instant-read digital thermometer to easily check the temperature while baking.

While microwaves remain quick and efficient heating devices, they are the bane of pot pies. Use the microwave only as a last resort to heat pot-pie leftovers, as it heats unevenly and will destroy tender homemade crusts, leaving soggy, unappetizing mush behind.

Check the internal temperature of a reheated pot pie before eating.

ALEXANDER HOFFMANN/SHUTTERSTOCK

The Big Chill

Perhaps the best way to store pot pies is by planning ahead and freezing your unbaked pies. They make perfect candidates for freezing as long as you follow some important guidelines.

WHAT FREEZES WELL

When freezing a pot-pie recipe for the first time, it is a good idea to freeze a test pie and consume it before stocking your freezer. The rigors of freezing and reheating are not suited for all pot pies.

Consider the type of pie that you are freezing; certain common

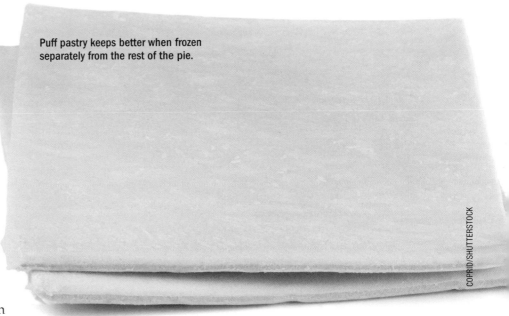

Puff pastry keeps better when frozen separately from the rest of the pie.

COPRID/SHUTTERSTOCK

Use the **microwave only as a last resort** to heat pot-pie leftovers, as it heats unevenly and will destroy tender homemade crusts, leaving soggy, unappetizing mush behind.

Aluminum foil helps leftovers retain moisture.

LASSE KRISTENSEN/SHUTTERSTOCK

ingredients, such as potatoes and celery, do not hold up well in a standard home freezer.

Do not attempt to freeze unbaked pot pies that include raw meats; this can cause a food-safety issue.

Pot pies featuring traditional pie crusts tend to handle freezing and reheating better than puff pastry or biscuit-dough toppings. If you prefer puff pastry on your pot pie, consider freezing the crust separately and adding the thawed dough on top just before baking.

The freezing process can affect the spicing of your pot pie by amplifying certain flavors or creating off-tastes. To prevent this issue, think about seasoning your dish lighter than normal.

THE FREEZING PROCESS

Freeze cooled, unbaked pies in metal pie pans or foil containers to avoid thermal shock when placed in a preheated oven.

Tightly cover unbaked pies in plastic wrap; then cover them again in one or two layers of foil.

For the best results, mark the pies with the date on which they were frozen, and bake them within one or two months of freezing. The only exception is if the pies are placed in a deep freezer, where they can last significantly longer.

THAWING AND COOKING

For even heating, defrost frozen pot pies in the refrigerator for at least 12 hours before baking. Make sure to remove the plastic wrap before cooking.

Bake at a moderate temperature of around 350 degrees F until the crust appears golden-brown and the internal temperature reaches 165 degrees F. If the crust begins to darken, lightly cover the top of the pie with a small sheet of foil while baking.

The amount of cooking time depends on the size of the pot pie. Small, individual pot pies typically need 20 to 30 minutes, and larger, multi-serving pies will need at least 40 to 50 minutes. If you take the pie directly from the freezer to the oven, be sure to allow for additional baking time.

Leftover or frozen homemade pot pies can provide delicious and nutritious meals on even the busiest of days, saving both time and money in the kitchen. By following these tips and tricks, leftovers won't be a dirty word again.

Kevin Fogle is a freelance writer and photographer based in South Carolina.

Easy and delicious, leftover pot pie can make an **additional meal or two** for your household.

Hops *and* Harmony

Pot pies and craft beers are a match made in heaven.

BY KEVIN FOGLE

while wine and food pairings traditionally dominate the culinary scene, beer pairings are an emerging trend across the country. The last two decades have seen a craft-beer renaissance in the United States, and most markets now stock domestic and international breweries that produce flavorful and varied beer styles. Both accessible and affordable, the flavors in the diverse family of ales and lagers have been shown to complement an even greater range of foods than wine, according to "The Oxford Companion to Beer" by Garrett Oliver (Oxford University Press).

KEVIN FOGLE

First brewed in England, India pale ales pair well with curry.

Poultry-based Pot Pies

Traditional chicken or turkey pot pies spiced with herbs such as thyme and fennel can be nicely paired with a Belgian farmhouse ale (also known as saison-style ales). These crisp, light-bodied ales offer a complex flavor that exudes herbal notes with light citrus highlights. Farmhouse ales work well with herb-based dishes and can cleanse the palette when paired with rich entrées such as pot pie. Great examples of this style include Saison Dupont brewed in Belgium and Hennepin by Brewery Ommegang based in New York.

A creamy citrus chicken pot pie might be served with an American India pale ale. American IPAs typically offer a hoppy flavor with bold floral and citrus notes, which complement the brightness of the lemon-and-chicken combination. Widely available American IPAs include the 60 Minute IPA from Dogfish Head Craft Brewery in Delaware and Two Hearted Ale from Bell's Brewery in Michigan.

A curry-based chicken pot pie ideally should be paired with a well-hopped beer such as a pale ale or an IPA. The bitterness of the hops from these styles both balance and enliven the complex flavors of any curry. Dale's Pale Ale from Oskar Blues Brewery in Colorado and Stone Pale Ale from Stone Brewing Co. in California make great choices for this pairing.

Craft beer is a great match for the versatile pot pie — no matter the ingredients or spicing — from a classic beef version to a spicy curry chicken dish. When pairing food with drink, you first want to examine the intensity of both the dish and the beer. Then select similar levels of strength to avoid overwhelming delicately flavored entrées with powerful beers or vice versa.

Next, consider complementing and contrasting flavor profiles between the food and the beer. Many pairings work when beers share a similar flavor with an aspect of the dish, while others try to emphasize interesting contrasts. As with all taste-based art forms, pairing foods with beer remains subjective, and multiple beer styles can be appropriate for every dish.

When pairing food with drink, you first want to **examine the intensity** of both the dish and the beer.

JESSE KUNERTH/SHUTTERSTOCK

If your favorite pot pie features turkey, you might want to pair it with a saison-style ale.

Beef pot pies can taste delicious with porter-style beers (right).

Beef-based Pot Pies

A very hearty meat dish, such as a beef and roasted mushroom pot pie, should be paired with a bold porter-style beer. The flavor of this full-bodied ale brings strong roasted notes with light coffee overtones that nicely complement the tender beef and earthiness of the mushrooms. Some of the best American porter-style beers include Anchor Porter by Anchor Brewing Co. in California and Robust Porter by Smuttynose Brewing Co. in New Hampshire.

Ham-based Pot Pies

Dark lagers offer the perfect accompaniment to a warm ham pot pie. These crisp medium-to light-bodied lagers are deceptive; their dark coloration belies the easy drinkability while featuring delicate roasted notes and a strong malt backbone. The saltiness of the ham cleverly contrasts the lager's malty sweetness. Session Black Lager by Full Sail Brewing Co. in Oregon and Samuel Adams Black Lager by The Boston Beer Co. in Massachusetts make great choices for this dish.

Many pairings work when beers share a **similar flavor** with an aspect of the dish, while others try to **emphasize interesting contrasts.**

Vegetable-based Pot Pies

A roasted root-vegetable pot pie pairs well with American and English brown ales. When tasting a brown ale, you will notice prominent caramel and nutty notes with only moderate bitterness from the hops. This flavor creates a nice balance with the crispy roasted edges of the potatoes or parsnips and their underlying sweetness. Good brown-ale examples include Hazelnut Brown Nectar from Rogue Ales in Oregon and Ellie's Brown Ale from Avery Brewing Co. in Colorado.

Any pot pies highlighting asparagus or Brussels sprouts are best matched with a Belgian-style tripel ale. The distinctive flavors of these vegetables harmonize well with big golden-colored tripel ales, which typically feature a complex blend of spicy and fruity notes with a warm finish from the high alcohol content. Allagash Tripel Ale from Allagash Brewing Co. in Maine and La Fin Du Monde from Unibroue in Quebec, Canada, offer excellent selections for this pairing.

When pairing beers with pot pie, there are no hard or fast rules to follow. Have fun, and experiment with new and different beer styles that might complement or contrast other aspects of your dish. There is a world of options waiting for you, so get creative, and pair away.

- -

Kevin Fogle is a freelance photographer, writer and home-brewer based in South Carolina.

Food for Thought

"There is nothing better on a cold, wintry day than a properly made pot pie."

– CRAIG CLAIBORNE (1920-2000),
American author, journalist and food critic